D1570994

In *Thirty-Three Ways Seven Faiths Agree With Meher Baba,* Tom Wolfe has gathered overwhelming evidence of commonalities among all faiths. A seeker of the truth reading this book will receive the clarity that there is unity and oneness behind all faiths, and this conviction will bring him the courage and longing to step further into the spiritual path.

Mehernoush McPherson

Tom Wolfe's study of how the largest religions throughout time agree with Meher Baba massages the feet of the old wise ones, once again awakening these oft-stated Truths by rubbing them one against another.

Bryan West

All religions, and all souls, are in fact one. When sunlight passes through a prism, it is refracted in a myriad colors, all beautifully different from each other, but their source is identical. Likewise, the teachings and truths of all the great incarnations of the Divine, and those of all the saints and the lovers of God, are fundamentally the same; they only appear different when seen only superficially through the mind and not felt in the depths of the heart. Jalaluddin Rumi, a Sufi mystic who lived many centuries ago, describes this truth with his characteristic humor:

> The roads are different, but the destination is one.
> All those who yelled at each other along the way,
> "You hypocrite! You infidel!" in the end,
> drink from the same keg of wine, and laugh out loud!

Jeff Wolverton

Thirty-Three Ways Seven Faiths Agree with Meher Baba

by Thomas Wolfe & Companions

Published by
Be Friendly Ministries

Hardcover Edition

Book and cover design by Karl Moeller.

ISBN: 978-1-7365226-1-5

Garamond font

First edition 2021.

BeFriendlyMinistries@gmail.com

Dedication

To Meher Baba, the God-Man,
who, through the depth of His silence,
allows us to feel REAL LOVE's way

To Hafiz of Shiraz, the Man-God,
who, through the depth of his unsurpassed words,
allows us to read of REAL LOVE's way

To you both,
One in God, do I this book dedicate, I dedicate!
My heart dedicates, for :

تنها تو هستی

Tanha Tow Hasti
You Alone Exist!

CONTENTS

CONTENTS

"Meher Baba, the White Horse Avatar," by Vanessa Weichberger (acrylic on canvas, 2021)

PREFACE

In *Thirty-Three Ways Seven Faiths Agree With Meher Baba*, we are invited to rise to the level of understanding that has been bequeathed to the world by the presence of the greatest Spiritual Masters. From Zarathushtra, the ancient Prophet of Persia, to Lord Krishna, the Avatar of Vishnu, as well as the Jewish wisdom of Tanakh, which came down to us through the lineage of Abraham, Isaac and Jacob, and Moses. From Lord Buddha, the Enlightened One, and Muhammad, the Prophet of Arabia (peace be upon Him and His family), and the marvelous Sufis as well.

From Yeshua, the Hebrew Prophet of Israel, now known the world over as our Lord Jesus Christ, and the faith that has become the Religious Society of Friends of Truth, or Quakers. The adventure set before us by Thomas Wolfe and his companions is indeed the quest of a lifetime: to seek and find the Jewel in the Lotus, and once apprehending the Truth, sharing Divine Love with one and all.

I started on this path in 1986, in New York City. I remember sitting in my college student lounge, waiting for my next class, and reading *God Speaks* by Meher Baba.

When the bell rang for my next class, I looked down at my book, and then over at the clock, and had to make a decision. Should I keep reading the wisdom of my Spiritual Master, or go to class? It was not an easy choice for me. Baba said:

> The religion that I shall give teaches the knowledge of the One behind the many. The book that I shall make people read is the book of the heart that holds the key to the mystery of life. I shall bring about a happy blending of the head and the heart. I shall revitalize all

1

religions and cults, and bring them together like beads on one string.*

Throughout His life Meher Baba lived this message of love and truth, and now that He has passed away many others are living it as well, recognizing that in the new millennium there is room for all points of view, room for all faiths, room for all ways back to God, as rivers return to the Ocean. The fact that God revealed the Truth to different people, at different times, in a magnificent series of manifestations is starting to sink in as self-evident. The old ways of clinging to exclusive narrow dogmas, which create separateness, are slowly dying off and providing room for living spiritual experience, which brings Oneness through love. Tom Wolfe has had such an experience and that is what inspired him to create this experience for you.

This book is yet another example of bringing the faiths together, in peace, mutual respect, tolerance, love, and sharing the beauty of the different perspectives and understanding each has to offer. It is clear that the "One behind the many" is God Himself, the Truth that is the string running through the core of each bead. For isn't the essence of each faith the same one Truth? And what is that Truth? Jesus said it clearly: "Love the Lord thy God with all thy heart and all thy might (mind). And love thy neighbor as thyself." And furthermore, God is also manifest here in the world as the Master.

All faiths know that God manifests and guides humanity ever closer, age after blessed age back to Him. How that manifestation occurs, and what we create based on the experience, is the subject of this book.

---

* Meher Baba, *God Speaks,* 2nd edition. (Walnut Creek, CA: Sufism Reoriented, 1973), pp. xxvi.

You are in for a wild ride, and I can pretty much guarantee that since you are holding this book in your hands, you will not be the same as a result of reading. And what result can we hope for? That all faiths, all people, live the message of the Masters, to love God and ultimately become one with God.

Laurent Weichberger
April 2020

Baba in Rahuri Cabin, lower Meherabad, ca. 1938

INTRODUCTION

How Be Friendly Ministries Began
Meherabad, India, 1988

My first trip to Meherabad, which is Meher Baba's main center in India, was in 1988. On the plane I got anxious that Meher Baba might not be a real Master. I had studied religion at the University of Pennsylvania, and our method of studying religion was to participate in the worship of each faith community, many of whom were underwhelming. So, I knew I would be heartbroken if Meher Baba turned out to be a false teacher.

When I met Meher Baba's *mandali* * I expected them to teach me about Meher Baba's message, but they were not interested in teaching at all. They wanted to know where you came from, how you found out about Meher Baba, could they get you a cup of tea. They were your servants, and that really showed me that Meher Baba manifested humility in those around him. I particularly connected with Mani, Meher Baba's sister, and Eruch, his right-hand man.

On the second day, after I had settled in, I was sitting in my room looking out the window, and I saw a cow about a football field away. Inside myself, I knew the cow was going to walk over to my window. I had the *Bhagavad Gita*, the *Qur'an*, the *Bible*, and *The Dhammpada* open on the desk. Internally, the question arose: "Could Meher Baba's messages of 'The Seven Realities,' 'How to Love God,' 'My Wish For My Lovers,' and 'Twelve Ways of Realizing Me,' be a frame for how to go through scripture to find common principles?"

In that moment, Be Friendly Ministries was born. If you consider these four messages Meher Baba gave out separately, there are seven realities, eight parts to "How to Love God,"

---

* A term most often applied by Meher Baba to those who live with Him, although Baba sometimes used the term to denote close disciples, those who were of His Circle.

six parts to "My Wish for My Lovers," and twelve ways of realizing, which add up to thirty-three principles.

At the time, I didn't think this idea was central to my life. I just thought it was an interesting so-called coincidence of events and thoughts. In the Quaker community, we call these "God-incidences," and it just felt like a personal God-incidence. Thirty years later, having contemplated the eleven religions of the Interfaith Conference of Washington, DC, where I was Treasurer for twelve years, I see that it is an incredibly perfect, comprehensive, easily understood framing of the spiritual path that anyone can participate in.

William Penn's Method and the Book Gift, 1997

I grew up Christian in the United Methodist Church and the Church of England. In fact, I was considering becoming clergy in the Church of England when I went to the University of Pennsylvania (UPenn). However, because of the Vietnam War, the fact that my family belonged to a military church, and the exclusiveness of the Christian creed, I could no longer self-identify as a Christian.

One day, at the rise of meeting at Adelphi Friends Monthly Meeting, a woman named Jane Furniss gave me *The Collected Works of William Penn*. It was a huge book, about 24x30 inches and 1,000 pages, and it was one of the original printings from 1728. She handed it to me and said, "I want you to have this because I know you're one of the few people who will actually read it."

So I sat right down in the sanctuary of Adelphi Friends Meeting and started reading. As God would have it, I opened right up to *The Sandy Foundation of Christianity Shaken*, which William Penn wrote when he was twenty-three years old. He printed 10,000 copies and distributed them throughout London at his own expense. What William Penn does in that small, thirty-page pamphlet is remove Christian exclusivity from the message that God's Light is within every person. Upon reading this pamphlet, I immediately, internally said to myself, "I can be a Christian by this definition because it doesn't exclude anybody." This epiphany was a huge moment because my inability to identify as a Christian had been painful for my family and me.

Back to William Penn: one week after publication and distribution of *The Sandy Foundation of Christianity Shaken*, Penn was condemned to death for heresy and imprisoned in the Tower of London for nine months. During that time, he wrote *No Cross, No Crown*, in which he perfected his method of going through scripture and finding examples of the inward light in every person. Specifically, he examined the Tanakh, the Jewish scripture, and multiple Greek philosophers, and he found examples of about thirty principles where they agreed that the light of God is accessible to every heart directly.

Jane Furniss was right—I am one of those people who read *The Collected Works of William Penn* cover to cover, and I realized that William Penn had perfected this method, called the synoptic method, of finding commonalities in different scriptures. When you talk about the "Synoptic Gospels," it means the Gospels of Mark, Matthew, and Luke, because they agree with each other. What I see Be Friendly Ministries doing is illustrating how the scripture of different religions are synoptic. The synoptic good news (which is what "gospel" means) is now the whole world of scripture rather than just Judeo-Christian scripture. As I read about the method William Penn had perfected in his lifetime, it fit perfectly with the idea I had in Meherabad in 1988. Be Friendly Ministries combines the method of William Penn with the principles of Meher Baba to create a comprehensive understanding of the consistency of God's news. Amen and Hallelujah!

Maryland Council of Social Studies

After five years of laboring together with eleven faith communities, the Interfaith Conference (IFC) of Metropolitan D.C. published the *Teaching About Religion (T.A.R.) Handbook*. We subsequently published three supplements on the following topics—symbols of each faith community, what they teach about the environment, and each faith's values. These publications are available on the IFC of Metropolitan D.C.'s website—ifcmw.org.

We tested the *T.A.R. Handbook* in Virginia, and Fairfax County bought dozens of copies. So we decided to take it to the Maryland Council of Social Studies convention in October 2000. Coincidentally, the National Council of Social Studies was having their national convention in early December in Washington, D.C. However, we decided not to participate in that convention until we found out if the *T.A.R. Handbook* was well received by the Maryland social studies teachers.

At the conference of Maryland social studies teachers, we were amazed and pleased that virtually every social studies teacher rejoiced that someone had done this work. The primary reason the social studies teachers find this work valuable is because they don't have to study the religion to teach it, as well as because each religion vetted their own chapter; therefore, the answers to the forty-four questions are completely authentic and referenced. It is therefore very easy for the social studies teachers to share this information with their students because all they have to do is compile the lesson plans.

One possible future project would be to collect these lesson plans into a meta-analysis because many social studies teachers created lesson plans to teach world religions from the *T.A.R. Handbook*.

My favorite part of the story: at about noon, when we realized we had a hit and we had sold dozens of the *T.A.R. Handbook* to enthusiastic social studies teachers from Maryland, D.C., Rao, one of the Hindu IFC board members, turned to me and said, "We really blew it."

Tom: "What do you mean we really blew it? We're getting incredible reception!"

D.C. Rao: "We really blew it by not signing up for the National Council of Social Studies Convention in early December."

I sadly agreed that it really should have gone to the national level, and the thought that it had to wait another year was disappointing.

The next person who walked into the booth was Susan Griffin, who recognized me.

She pointed at me and said, "You used to be on the board of William Penn House."

And I said, "Yes I did."

She said, "I am the Executive Director of the National Council of Social Studies teachers, and is there any way I can help you with this work?"

D.C. Rao turned to me and said, "Well, I guess we have to let God do His part in this work, too." We told Susan the story of how we had been shortsighted in not signing up for the National Council of Social Studies. Susan pulled out her phone, called her administrative assistant, got us a booth, and reduced the cost of the booth by half. It was an amazing God-incidence. It sends chills up and down my spine just remembering that moment.

Saudis at the State Department

In 2010 I received a phone call: "Mr. Wolfe, this is the State Department. Would you be willing to meet with a delegation from Saudi Arabia?"

I was convinced it was some friend of mine goofing on me, so I said, "Sure, I'm the President of the United States, I'll meet with you whenever you want. Ha ha ha."

The voice on the phone said, "No, Mr. Wolfe, this really is the State Department of the United States, and we want you to come downtown and meet with a delegation from Saudi Arabia that has asked for you and Imam Johari Abdul Malik specifically to meet with them."

It turns out that the Saudi educators had found out that we were teaching Islam in the public school system of the United States again, and they wanted to vet how we were teaching their religion. So Imam Johari Abdul Malik and I decided to go to speak to a delegation of eighteen men from the higher levels of education in the Kingdom of Saudi Arabia.

When the Jewish members of the IFC Board found out we were going to meet with the Saudi delegation, they insisted that we had to look at what the Saudis taught about Jews in their textbooks. I have to admit I was convinced the Jewish members of the IFC were overreacting, partially because a man I had met and admired, Cat Stevens, was being challenged as a representative singer for the annual IFC concert, which happens every November. Because of the Jewish board members' challenge to Cat Stevens (who had converted to Islam) singing at the concert, I believed they were probably overreacting to the textbooks of the Saudis.

Johari and I got copies of the textbooks, which were available online. We were shocked to see that the teaching of hatred from elementary school through high school was well documented both in Arabic and in English. Johari and I made twenty-five copies of the textbooks in both Arabic and English and decided to confront the delegation from Saudi Arabia about the hatred of Jews and Christians in their textbooks. We decided to honor the ancient Quaker maxim, "It's easier to ask for forgiveness than permission," and we did not inform the State Department of our plan.

At our three-hour meeting at the State Department, I was the only person in the room who did not speak fluent Arabic. The State Department provided two interpreters, and Johari and I presented how we were teaching Islam in the public school system, which the Saudis celebrated. They were very pleased with the depth and accuracy with which we represented their religion in the *T.A.R. Handbook*. I also shared with them that William Penn was condemned to death for teaching, among other things, that the light of God was in Muslims in 1668. The Saudis were shocked and very pleasantly surprised that at least one denomination of Christianity did not exclude Islam from the light of God.

After an hour of celebrating with the Saudis about the chapter of Islam in the *T.A.R. Handbook*, we verbally challenged their teaching of hatred of Jews in their textbooks to the very young through young adults. The Saudis insisted that they loved Yehudi and that there wasn't a problem. We then pulled out the eighty-page document of the actual textbooks used in the Saudi educational system and gave each member of the delegation and the interpreters a copy. I felt concern for the State Department representative who, once he saw what we were doing, realized that there was a potential for conflict.

Over the next hour and a half to two hours, we had a vibrant and forthright dialogue with the Saudi educators concerning teaching about other religions and demonizing other religions. Imam Johari and I shared with them a *tafsir*, which is a scriptural analysis of the *Qur'an* that celebrated the Jewish prophets and clearly showed that the *Qur'an* teaches interfaith respect and a strong admiration for the Jewish prophets.

There were some amazing moments in that two-hour conversation. One of the amazing moments was when Imam Johari mentioned that the Jews keep the Sabbath. It became obvious after three references to the Jewish Sabbath that not a single Saudi in the room could conceive of the Jewish people keeping a holy day of rest and worship. Johari and I were stunned. Later we said it was like trying to explain snow to a desert dweller; the Saudis just couldn't conceive that the Jewish people had a Sabbath.

Both Johari and I got the sense in our prayer and reflection later that the educators from Saudi Arabia are not where the problem lies. We found the educators very comfortable and respectful with the concept of celebrating the many, many passages in the *Qur'an* that celebrate the Jewish faith and prophets. In fact, we had two subsequent meetings with the Saudi delegations. During the second meeting, we met with the two heads of the Qur'anic Memorization Society, which is an organization that has taught 160,000 undergraduates to memorize the *Qur'an*. These men can sing any *surah* (chapter) of the *Qur'an*. They sang a dozen different *surahs* that celebrate David, Moses, Abraham, Jacob, Ishmael, and Isaac. They sang these *surahs* with their entire heart and a big smile on their face. What we did during the second meeting made it even more obvious that the educators were willing to celebrate the Jewish faith and prophets.

Subsequently, I presented this story to the American Jewish Committee. On the way back from that presentation I realized I had to stop doing this work, because it was so stressful and hate-filled, and there needed to be a larger organization that provided support to people who choose to do this work. Interestingly enough, Imam Johari came to the same conclusion the same week, and we both stopped working with the *T.A.R. Handbook* project.

The interaction with the Saudi educators showed me how misunderstanding and misrepresentation are entrenched in comparative religion within our faith communities. In the case of the Saudis it is institutionalized into the education system and not just isolated to the houses of worship. Now, years later, I am deeply struck by remembering the events of those three meetings with the Saudi educators. What William Penn and Meher Baba have made simply obvious will not be simply obvious as a blessing to those still influenced by the teaching of hatred.

The television program *60 Minutes* broadcast an interview of a five-year-old Saudi girl, and she was asked, "What do you think about Jews?"

She replied, "We should kill them all," which took the interviewer aback.

He then asked, "Why? Why would you say that?"

She said, "Well, we know from the *Qur'an* that the *Quimat* (Apocaplyse) won't come and we won't all go to heaven until all the Jews are dead."

The Unity of the Good News, 2001

In 2001, I was at work at my business, Smile Herb Shop, and I had an intuition to go home to my prayer gazebo for a message. In the five minutes it took me to get home, I felt more and more strongly that there was definitely a message. So I went out to the prayer gazebo; within an hour of prayer, there was this golden light, the most amazing thing, in the gazebo, and the message was very simple: "The unity of the good news has been restored." The message repeated three times. It was clear to me that my calling in life was to live up to that message and to help other people understand that, as William Penn says, "There is not a nation in this world nor an age throughout all time that has been destitute of the discovery of inward light."

While this was happening, my first wife Linda heard that there was a tornado watch but she decided not to disturb me. It was the first tornado watch in College Park in eighty-five years. We didn't think much of it until the next day when we went out and saw the destruction the tornado had wrought on College Park, which had happened simultaneously as I received the message: "The unity of the good news has been restored." I have no idea what to make of this combination of events, but that's what happened. From then on I knew that part of God's reality in my heart was that the unity of the good news had been restored.

Katherine Peck Story

I was in the Refectory at the Meher Spiritual Center in Myrtle Beach, South Carolina, doing one of my favorite activities. I discovered a cookbook called *The Quaker Baker*, and I love to bake for people, particularly in religious retreat settings. I had spent the previous day baking with a lovely woman named Katherine Peck. She had heard me discussing Be Friendly Ministries and saying we use the method of William Penn and thirty-three Principles of Meher Baba, and she let me know she was a Quaker. I said, "Aww, two Quakers in the kitchen." I added, "Well, I'm the Clerk of Ministry and Worship at Annapolis Friends Meeting."

She said, "Oh! I'm the Clerk of Ministry and Worship at Celo Friends Meeting in the mountains of North Carolina!"

I then said, "As you know, it has been a long time since unprogrammed Quakers have recorded ministry, and I have applied to embrace and possibly record my ministry at Annapolis Friends Meeting."

She then said, "Oh! As you know, Celo Friends Meeting is a member of Southern Appalachian Yearly Meeting, and Southern Appalachian Yearly Meeting has not recorded ministry for decades as well, and we just recorded our first minister, Geeta McGaughy, a medical doctor who is doing a ministry on the environment, a traveling ministry from Quaker meeting to Quaker meeting. Would you like me to send you the committee's minutes on how we recorded ministry for the first time in decades?"

It was just a coincidence, of course, that her committee had done the work that the Ministry and Worship Committee at Annapolis Friends Meeting was about to embark on. Then she said (it was her first visit to the Meher Center), "I am beginning to believe there might be something to this Meher Baba fellow."

The Al Nur Mosque

I am the co-chair of the Greater Annapolis Interfaith Network, and we have community programs on the second Thursday of every month. We had scheduled the Annapolis Immigration Justice Network (AIJN) to hold a program on the second Thursday of March 2019, which was the 15th. Understandably, given the horrific state of immigration policy, AIJN was overwhelmed and had to cancel their scheduled program at the last minute.

So I decided, on the spur of the moment, to do a program about "The Unity of the Good News." It was a delightful sharing, and I again felt God's guidance and loving hand in this ministry.

The next morning during a business meeting, my administrative assistant asked me if I knew what had happened in New Zealand. She shared with me the horrible murder of fifty-one Muslims at the Al Nur Mosque and

Al-Nur Mosque, Christchurch, New Zealand

Linwood Islamic Center that had happened the day before. We shared a few tears and then held our business meeting.

The next morning during my prayer and meditation time, the question kept coming up: "What time was it in Christchurch, New Zealand, when the incident occurred?" Three times this question came up.

New Zealand is eighteen hours ahead of Eastern Standard Time. When preparations began for our program at 6:30 pm EST, it was 2:30 pm in New Zealand, which was exactly the height of the intensity of the assault on the two mosques.

My heart knew this was not a coincidence, and I again felt God's *nazar* (loving gaze and guidance) on this ministry. Friends, it was the same moment in time that the extreme nature of the problem presented itself, as well as the solution.

Unity of the Good News Restored, 2020

An attorney friend and I were having a delightful dinner in an upscale restaurant in Myrtle Beach, South Carolina. I was describing with enthusiasm the momentum that Be Friendly Ministries was gathering within the Quaker and Meher Baba communities to show God's faithfulness and consistency over the past 4,000 years.

Our waiter William, coming and going, approached the table: "May I ask you a question about religion?"

"Sure," I said, aware that this does not usually happen in the middle of fine dining.

William said, "My pastor says Muhammad is sent from Satan. Do you believe Muhammad is sent from the Devil?"

I shared with William the story of my mother's funeral, during which the United Methodist clergyman and I stood in two pulpits and shared fourteen praises of Jesus, each one followed by the other pulpit exclaiming in celebration: " Isn't scripture wonderful!" After fourteen praises of Jesus, I praised one last time, "Isn't scripture wonderful!"

William was as surprised as my conservative Christian relatives from North Carolina to hear that all of the fourteen praises of Jesus came from the *Qur'an*. He asked that I send him the fourteen quotes praising Jesus from the *Qur'an*; I offered instead to send him a draft of a planned booklet from Be Friendly Ministries, *Thirty-Three Ways Muhammad Agrees with Jesus.*

We were the last diners to leave the restaurant, and William shared with us his humble knowing: "It just doesn't make sense to me that hundreds of millions of people are following Satan." My beloved wife called it to my attention and my heart was struck by the fact that often the laity is wiser about separation than the clergy.

Meher Baba at Pune Center

SECTION ONE

PROPER UNDERSTANDING

THE SEVEN REALITIES

Meher Baba gives no importance to creed, dogma, caste systems, and the performance of religious ceremonies and rites, but to the UNDERSTANDING of the following seven Realities.

Avatar Meher Baba, Meherabad, India, 1927

PRINCIPLE 1

OUR REAL EXISTENCE
IS ONENESS

1. The only REAL EXISTENCE is that of the One and only God, Who is the Self in every (finite) self.

Meher Baba:

> All souls (atmas) were, are and will be in the Over-Soul (Paramatma). Souls (atmas) are all One.
>
> Most souls have great binding; some souls have little binding; a few souls have very little binding; and a very few souls have absolutely no binding.
>
> All these souls (atmas) of different consciousness, of different experiences, of different states are in the Over-Soul (Paramatma) … and all are One.

> Meher Baba, *God Speaks*, 2nd edition. (Walnut Creek, CA: Sufism Reoriented, 1973), pp. 1–2.

Zarathushtra (Zoroastrianism):

> All Holy Lives are put into Thy hands,
> All that have been, and all that are today,
> And all, Oh God, that ever shall be.

> Irach J.S. Taraporewala, *The Divine Songs of Zarathushtra*, 3rd edition. (Mumbai, India: Hukhta Foundation, 2014), Ahunavaiti 6.10—Yasna 33:10.

Krishna (Hinduism):

I am the Self, Arjuna,
seated in the heart of all beings;
I am the beginning and the life span
of beings, and their end as well.

Bhagavad Gita. Translated by Stephen Mitchell. (New
York, NY: Three Rivers Press, 2000), 10.20.

When he sees that the myriad beings
emanate from the One
and have their source in the One,
that man gains absolute freedom.

This supreme Self is beginningless,
deathless, and unconfined;
although it inhabits bodies,
it neither acts nor is tainted.

Bhagavad Gita. 13.30–31.

Tanakh (Jewish Scriptures):

You will know and believe in Me, and understand that I
am He; before Me nothing was created by a god, nor will
there be after Me!

Tanach, The Stone Edition. (Brooklyn, NY: Mesorah
Publications, Ltd., 2011), Isaiah 43:10.

It has been clearly demonstrated to you that the Lord alone is God; there is none beside Him.

Tanakh: The Holy Scriptures, New JPS Translation. (Jerusalem: The Jewish Publication Society, 1985), Deuteronomy 4:35.

Buddha (Buddhism):

Because of Ignorance (avidya) the principle of individuation as discriminated from Enlightenment which is the principle of unity and sameness the primal unity becomes divided into thinking, thinker and discriminated thoughts by reason of which there appear the "formations" of karma.

A Buddhist Bible. Edited by Dwight Goddard. (Boston, MA: Beacon Press, 1970), p. 645.

Jesus (Christianity):

… But to us there is but one God, the Father, of whom are all things, and we in him.

Authorized (King James) Version (AV). (Nashville, TN: Thomas Nelson, 2016), 1 Corinthians 8:4–6 (AV).

And Jesus answered him, "The first of all the commandments is, Hear, O Israel; The Lord our God is one Lord: And thou shalt love the Lord thy God with all thy heart, and with all thy soul, and with all thy mind, and with all thy strength: this is the first commandment."

Mark 12:29–30 (AV).

Muhammad's Revelation (Islam)*:

All praise is due to God alone, the Sustainer of all the worlds, the Most Gracious, the Dispenser of Grace, Lord of the Day of Judgment! Thee alone do we worship, and unto Thee alone do we turn for aid.

The Qur'an. Translated and explained by Muhammad Asad. (London, England: The Book Foundation, 2003), Al-Fatihah (The Opening) 1:2–5.

This is a message unto all mankind. Hence, let them be warned thereby, and let them know that He is the One and Only God; and let those who are endowed with insight take this to heart!

The Qur'an. Ibrāhīm (Abraham) 14:52.

Quakers:

I saw that Christ enlightens all men and women with His divine and saving Light. I saw that the grace of God, which brings salvation has appeared to all men, and that the manifestation of God was given to every man to profit withal.

George Fox, *The Journal of George Fox*, "A Spiritual Worship," 1649. (London, J.M. Dent & Sons, 1924), p. 21.

---

*It is important to know that in Islamic belief, Muhammad did not write the Holy *Qur'an*, he transcribed it from visions given to him by Allah through the angel Gabriel. In other faith traditions, we may refer to the Prophet as being the author of a scriptural quote. For Islam, however, we refer to "Muhammad's Revelation" rather than Muhammad himself. This is an essential distinction in the way that Islam views the difference between Allah and the Prophet Muhammad and can help us understand some of the key theological arguments between Islam and Christianity.

Therefore I say, preach your Truth; let it go forth, and you will find, without any notable miracle, as of old, that everyone will speak in their own tongue, in which they were born. And I will say that if these pure principles have their place in us and are brought forth by faithfulness and obedience into practice, the difficulties and doubts that we might have to surmount will be easily conquered. There will be a power higher than these. Let it be called The Great Spirit of the Indian, the Quaker's "Inward Light" of George Fox, the blessed "Mary, Mother of Jesus" of the Catholics: or Brahma, the Hindu's God—they will all be one, and there will come to be such faith and such liberty as shall redeem the world.

Lucretia Mott, *Lucretia Mott Speaks: The Essential Speeches and Sermons*, "To the Free Religious Association," 1873. (Chicago, Illinois: University of Illinois Press, 2017), p. 204.

Ke kim ya'ye sa'a'dat ra figh bud ra'figh
Beh ma ma'ni ro'o for'sat sho'mor gha'nimas'te vaght

Regret and sorrow that up to this time I knew not,
That the alchemy of happiness is ever the Friend, the Friend!

Hafiz

PRINCIPLE 2

LOVE IS THE LONGING TO KNOW MORE AND IMPROVE OURSELVES

2. The only REAL LOVE is the Love for this Infinity (God), which arouses an intense longing to see, know, and become one with its Truth (God).

Meher Baba:

> The sojourn of the soul is a thrilling divine romance in which the lover—who in the beginning is conscious of nothing but emptiness, frustration, superficiality, and the gnawing chains of bondage—gradually attains an increasingly fuller and freer expression of love. And ultimately the lover disappears and merges in the divine Beloved to realize the unity of the lover and the Beloved in the supreme and eternal fact of God as infinite Love.
>
> Meher Baba, *Discourses*, revised 6th edition. (North Myrtle Beach, SC: Sheriar Foundation, 2007), vol. III, p. 189.

Zarathushtra:

> Led by the Holy Spirit to the Best,
> His tongue shall utter only words of Love.
>
> *The Divine Songs of Zarathushtra.* Spenta-Mainyu 1.2—Yasna 47.2.

Through Knowledge's Wisdom grant me Inner Strength,
And all-embracing Love through Love.

The Divine Songs of Zarathushtra. Ahunavaiti 6:12—Yasna
33:12.

Krishna:

Whoever, clear-minded, knows me
as the Ultimate Person, knows
all that is truly worth knowing,
and he loves me with all his heart.

Bhagavad Gita. 15.19.

Concentrate your mind on me,
fill your heart with my presence,
love me, serve me, worship me,
and you will attain me at last.

Bhagavad Gita. 9.34.

Tanakh:

[God continues:] And I have loved you with an eternal
love, therefore I have extended kindness to you.

Tanach, The Stone Edition. Jeremiah 31:2.

He loves what is right and just;
the earth is full of the Lord's faithful care.

Tanakh: The Holy Scriptures. Psalms 33:5.

Buddha:

> Whether we see it or fail to see it, it is manifest always
> and everywhere....
> Take your stand on this, and the rest will follow of its
> own accord;
> To trust in the Heart is the Not Two, the Not Two is to
> trust in the Heart.
> I have spoken, but in vain; for what can words tell
> Of things that have no yesterday, tomorrow or today?

> *Buddhist Texts Through the Ages,* Edward Conze, ed.
> Attributed to Takakusu XLVIII, 376, translated by
> Arthur Waley. (New York: Philosophical Library, 1954),
> pp. 297–298.

Jesus:

> Jesus said unto him, "Thou shalt love the Lord thy God
> with all thy heart, and with all thy soul, and with all thy
> mind. This is the first and great commandment. And the
> second is like unto it, Thou shalt love thy neighbour as
> thyself. On these two commandments hang all the law
> and the prophets."

> Matthew 22:37–40 (AV).

> "He that hath my commandments, and keeps them, he it
> is that loveth me: and he that loveth me shall be loved by
> my Father, and I will love him, and will manifest myself
> to him."

> John 14:21 (AV).

Muhammad's Revelation:

Verily, those who attain to faith and do righteous deeds
will the Most Gracious endow with love: and only to
this end have we made this [divine writ] easy to
understand, in thine own tongue, [O Prophet,] so that
thou might convey thereby a glad tiding to the God-
conscious.

The Qu'ran. Marayam (Mary) 19:96–97.

Quakers:

And yet Paul has no hesitation in asserting that he
conquered sin and the enemies of the Soul by sensing
and feeling God's holy power and being under Love's
domain. In Romans 8:38–39 Paul says: I am convinced
that there is nothing in death or life, in the realm of
spirits or superhuman powers, in the world as it is or the
world as it shall be, in the forces of the universe, in
heights or depths—nothing in all of creation that can
separate us from the Love of God in Jesus Christ.

Robert Barclay, *Barclay's Apology*, "Proposition IX," 1679.
(Newberg, Oregon: The Barclay Press, 1998), p. 169.

Michaelangelo's "Pieta," Rome, Italy

PRINCIPLE 3

SELF-SACRIFICE

3. The only Real Sacrifice is that in which, in pursuance of this Love, all things, body, mind, position, welfare, and even life itself are sacrificed.

Meher Baba:

> No sacrifice is too big to set man free from spiritual bondage and help him to inherit the Truth, which alone shall bring abiding peace to all and which alone will sustain an unassailable sense of universal fellowhood— cemented by the ungrudging love of all, for all, as expressions of the same Reality.

> Meher Baba, *Discourses*, revised 6th edition, vol. III, p. 105.

> The aspirant is always willing to offer everything for the divine Beloved, and no sacrifice is too difficult for him. All his thoughts are turned away from the self and come to be exclusively centered on the divine Beloved.

> Meher Baba, *Discourses*, revised 6th edition, vol. I, p. 167.

Zarathushtra:

> That Holy-Word of Sacrifice went forth
> From God—one with Eternal Law;
> God Himself hath in this Word ordained
> The sweets of Mother-Earth to all who serve.

The Divine Songs of Zarathushtra. Ahunavaiti 1.7—Yasna 29.7.

> When She appeals for every open doubt,
> Or when, O God, secret ones She solves;
> Or when for mere trifling lapse a man
> To long and dire penances submits;—
> All this Thou watchest with Thy radiant Eye,
> And close observ'st, as laid down in Thy Law.

The Divine Songs of Zarathushtra. Ahunavaiti 4.13—Yasna 31.13.

Krishna:

> If this is beyond your powers,
> dedicate yourself to me;
> performing all actions for my sake,
> you will surely achieve success.

Bhagavad Gita. 12.10.

> The whole world becomes a slave
> to its own activity, Arjuna;
> if you want to be truly free,
> perform all actions as worship.

Bhagavad Gita. 3.9.

Tanakh:

> True sacrifice to God is a contrite spirit;
> God, You will not despise
> a contrite and crushed heart.

Tanakh: The Holy Scriptures. Psalms 51:19.

Buddha:

> Come, look at this glittering world, like unto a royal chariot; the foolish are immersed in it, but the discerning do not cling to it.

The Dhammapada. Translated by Irving Babbitt. (New York, NY: New Directions Books, 1965). 13:171.

> One should not therefore hold anything dear. Its loss is grievous. Those who hold nothing dear and hate nothing have no fetters.

The Dhammapada. 16:211.

Jesus:

> And to love him with all the heart, and with all the understanding, and with all the soul, and with all the strength, and to love his neighbour as himself, is more than all whole burnt offerings and sacrifices. And when Jesus saw that he answered discreetly, he said unto him, "Thou art not far from the kingdom of God." And no man after that durst ask him any question.

Mark 12:33–34 (AV).

But to do good and to communicate forget not: for with such sacrifices God is well pleased.

Hebrews 13:16 (AV).

Muhammad's Revelation:

All who buy the life of this world at the price of the life to come – their suffering shall not be lightened, nor shall they be succoured!

The Qur'an. Al-Baqarah (The Cow) 2:86.

Quakers:

At another place I heard some of the magistrates say among themselves that had they enough money they would hire me to be their minister. This was where they did not well understand us and our principles; but when I heard of it I said, "it is time for me to be gone; for if their eye is so much to me or any of us, they will not come to their own teacher."

George Fox, *The Journal of George Fox*, "Meetings with Indians," 1650. P. 291.

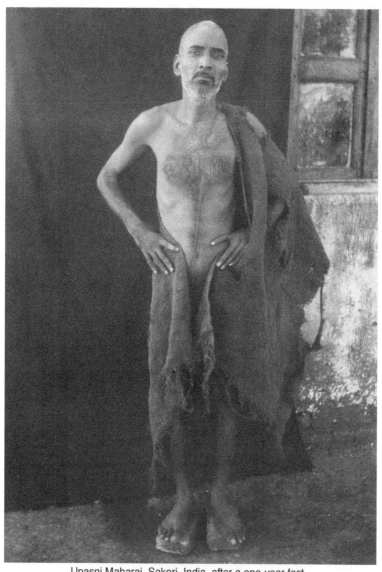

Upasni Maharaj, Sakori, India, after a one-year fast

PRINCIPLE 4

RENUNCIATION OF ALL SELFISH THOUGHTS AND DESIRES

4. The only Real Renunciation is that which abandons, even in the midst of worldly duties, all selfish thoughts and desires.

Meher Baba:

> Spirituality does not require the external renunciation of worldly activities or the avoiding of duties and responsibilities. It only requires that, while performing the worldly activities or discharging the responsibilities arising from the specific place and position of the individual, the inner spirit should remain free from the burden of desires.

Meher Baba, *Discourses*, revised 6th edition, vol. I, p. 20.

Zarathushtra:

> Thy Holy Spirit frustrates Evil Ones,
> But not, O God, any Truthful Man;
>> A man of small possessions here below
>> Inclines unto the Truth, but he who hath
>> Great riches is unfortunate, O Lord.

The Divine Songs of Zarathushtra. Spenta-Mainyu 1.4—Yasna 47.4.

God, Thou hast laid down that man shall choose
The Path of Truth and thus frustrate Untruth;
The Path of Truth is but the Path of Love,
Therefore, should man commune with Love,
And should renounce all contact with Untruth.

The Divine Songs of Zarathushtra. Spenta-Mainyu 3.3—Yas. 49.3.

Krishna:

When a man gives up all desires
that emerge from the mind, and rests
contented in the Self by the Self,
he is called a man of firm wisdom.

Bhagavad Gita. 2.55.

The true renunciate neither
desires things nor avoids them;
indifferent to pleasure and pain,
he is easily freed from all bondage.

Bhagavad Gita. 5.3.

Tanakh:

[Josiah] did what was pleasing to the Lord, following the ways of his father David without deviating to the right or to the left.

Tanakh: The Holy Scriptures. 2 Chronicles 34:2.

<u>Buddha:</u>

What now is the Noble Truth of the Extinction of
Suffering? It is the complete fading away and extinction
of this craving, its forsaking and giving up, the liberation
and detachment from it.
But where may this craving vanish, where may it be
extinguished? Wherever in the world there are delightful
and pleasurable things, there this craving may vanish,
there it may be extinguished.

A Buddhist Bible. P. 31.

<u>Jesus:</u>

There hath no temptation taken you but such as is
common to man: but God is faithful, who will not
suffer you to be tempted above that ye are able; but will
with the temptation also make a way to escape, that ye
may be able to bear it.

1 Corinthians 10:13 (AV).

Blessed is the man that endureth temptation: for when
he is tried, he shall receive the crown of life, which the
Lord hath promised to them that love him. Let no man
say when he is tempted, I am tempted of God: for God
cannot be tempted with evil, neither tempteth he any
man: But every man is tempted, when he is drawn away
of his own lust, and enticed.

James 1:12–14 (AV).

Muhammad's Revelation:

> ... people whom neither [worldly] commerce nor striving after gain can divert from the remembrance of God, and from constancy in prayer, and from charity.

> *The Qur'an.* An-Nur (The Light) 24:37.

> And thus have We willed you to be a community of the middle way, so that [with your lives] you might bear witness to the truth before all mankind.

> *The Qur'an.* Al-Baqarah (The Cow) 2:143.

Quakers:

> A blessed heavenly meeting this was; a powerful thundering testimony for Truth was borne there, a great sense there was among the people, and much brokenness and tenderness among them.

> George Fox, *The Journal of George Fox,* "Across the Bay to Maryland," 1655. P. 297.

> All Christians ought to be circumcised by the Spirit, which puts off the body of the sins of the flesh, that they may come to eat of the heavenly sacrifice, Christ Jesus, that true spiritual food, which none can rightly feed upon but that they are circumcised by the spirit.

> George Fox, 1649, *The Journal of George Fox,* "Fox and Children's Training," 1649. P. 34.

A'du cho tigh ka'shad amn se'par bi'yan'da'zam
Ke ti'ghe ma be'joz az na'le'I'yo a'hi nist

When the enemy Iblis (Satan), full of fraud, man seducing,
Draws his sword, we cast away the shield,
For save weeping and wailing, our sword is none.

Hafiz

PRINCIPLE 5

KNOWLEDGE IS EQUALITY AND NONJUDGMENT

5. The only Real Knowledge is the Knowledge that God is the inner dweller in good people and so-called bad, in saint and so-called sinner. This Knowledge requires you to help all equally as circumstances demand, without expectation of reward, and when compelled to take part in a dispute, to act without the slightest trace of enmity or hatred; to try to make others happy with brotherly or sisterly feeling for each one; to harm no one in thought, word, or deed, not even those who harm you.

Meher Baba:

> Selfless service is accomplished when there is not the slightest thought of reward or result, and when there is complete disregard of one's own comfort or convenience or the possibility of being misunderstood. When you are wholly occupied with the welfare of others, you can hardly think of yourself. You are not concerned with your comfort and convenience or your health and happiness. On the contrary you are willing to sacrifice everything for their well-being. Their comfort is your convenience, their health is your delight, and their happiness is your joy. You find your life in losing it in theirs. You live in their hearts, and your heart becomes their shelter. When there is true union of hearts, you completely identify yourself with the other person. Your act of help or word of comfort supplies to others whatever might be lacking in them; and

through their thoughts of gratitude and goodwill, you actually receive more than you give.

Meher Baba, *Discourses*, revised 6th edition, vol. I, p. 79.

Zarathushtra:

> Whatever deeds or words lift up the Mind
> Or lower it,—the Self shall follow sure;—
>> The choice once made, the Inner Will accepts
>> The Mind as guide, for better or for worse;
>> Thy Wisdom makes their destinies distinct.

The Divine Songs of Zarathushtra. Spenta-Mainyu 2.4—Yasna 48.4.

Krishna:

> When he sees all beings as equal
> in suffering or in joy
> because they are like himself,
> that man has grown perfect in yoga.

Bhagavad Gita. 6.32.

> He who sees that the great Lord
> is equally in all beings,
> deathless when every being
> dies—that man sees truly.

Bhagavad Gita. 13.27.

Tanakh:

> If your enemy is hungry, give him bread to eat;
> If he is thirsty, give him water to drink.

Tanakh: The Holy Scriptures. Proverbs 25:21.

Buddha:

> As the mind progresses towards Enlightenment, it
> becomes aware of clearing insight and sensitiveness as to
> the essential unity of all animate life, and there awakens
> within him a great heart of compassion and sympathy
> drawing all animate life together, harmonizing
> differences, unifying all dualisms.

The Buddhist Bible. P. 653.

> There is no path through the air; no (true) monk is
> found outside (the Buddhist Order). Nought in the
> phenomenal world abides, but the Awakened (the
> Buddhas) are never shaken.

The Dhammapada. 18:255.

Jesus:

> "This is my commandment, That ye love one another, as
> I have loved you.
> Greater love hath no man than this, that a man lay down
> his life for his friends."

John 15:12–13 (AV).

He that loveth his brother abideth in the light, and there is none occasion of stumbling in him.

1 John 2:10 (AV).

Muhammad's Revelation:

[And then,] behold, they shall be asked, "How is it that [now] you cannot succour one another?

The Qur'an. As-Saffatt (Those Ranged in Ranks) 37:24–25.

Those who are patient in adversity, and true to their word, and truly devout, and who spend [in God's way], and pray for forgiveness from their innermost hearts.

The Qur'an. Ãl-Imrãn (The House of Imrãn) 3:17.

Quakers:

Moreover I was brought up into His image in righteousness and holiness, and into the paradise of God. For of all the sects in Christendom (so called) that I discoursed with, I found none that could bear to be told that any should come to Adam's perfection, into that image of God that Adam was in before he fell; to be clear and pure without sin as he was.

George Fox, The Journal of George Fox, "Christ Fulfills all Types," 1665. P. 19.

Ha'fez'a tar'ke ja'han gof'tan ta'ri'ghe khosh'de'list,
Ta na'pen'da'ri ke ahva'le ja'han'daran khosh ast.

Hafiz! Abandoning the world is the path of
happy-heartedness,
So long as thou thinkest not that the circumstance of
World Possessors is pleasant.

Hafiz

PRINCIPLE 6

REAL CONTROL IS
DISCIPLINE OF THE SENSES

6. The only Real Control is the discipline of the senses from indulgence in low desires, which alone ensures absolute purity of character.

Meher Baba:

> Control of the habitual tendencies of the mind is much more difficult than control of physical actions. The fleeting and evasive thoughts and desires of the mind can be curbed only with great patience and persistent practice. But the restraint of mental processes and reactions is necessary to check the formation of new *sanskaras* * and to wear out or unwind the old *sanskaras* of which they are expressions. Though control might be difficult at the beginning, through sincere effort it gradually becomes natural and easy to achieve.

> Meher Baba, *Discourses*, revised 6th edition, vol. I, p. 72.

> The mind must turn away from all temptations, and complete control must be established over the senses. Thus control and dispassion are both necessary to attain one-pointedness in the search for true understanding.

> Meher Baba, *Discourses*, revised 6th edition, vol. III, p. 126.

---

* Impressions; traces or imprints of former experiences left as residue on consciousness that determines one's desires and actions.

Zarathushtra:

> But, God, he who through the urge of heart,
> Through sacrifice of Self, doth link himself,
> And his own Inner Self with Love,
> > Finds Wisdom, and Knowledge's Wisdom, too;
> > Sheltered by Righteousness, he shall dwell with Them.

The Divine Songs of Zarathushtra. Spenta-Mainyu 3.5—
Yasna 49.5.

Krishna:

> But the man who is self-controlled,
> who meets the objects of the senses
> with neither craving nor aversion,
> will attain serenity at last.

> In serenity, all his sorrows
> disappear at once, forever;
> when his heart has become serene,
> his understanding is steadfast.

Bhagavad Gita. 2.64–65.

> The superior man is he
> whose mind can control his senses;
> with no attachment to results,
> he engages in the yoga of action.

Bhagavad Gita. 3.6–7.

Tanakh:

> O Lord, remember in David's favor
>> his extreme self-denial,
>> how he swore to the Lord,
>> vowed to the Mighty One of Jacob,
>> "I will not enter my house,
>> nor will I mount my bed,
>> I will not give sleep to my eyes,
>> or slumber to my eyelids
>> until I find a place for the Lord,
>> an abode for the Mighty One of Jacob."

Tanakh: The Holy Scriptures. Psalms 132:1–5.

Buddha:

> 'All existing things are unreal.' He who knows and
> perceives this is no longer [in] the thrall of grief.

The Dhammapada. 20:279.

Jesus:

> For he that soweth to his flesh shall of the flesh reap
> corruption; but he that soweth to the Spirit shall of the
> Spirit reap life everlasting.

Galatians 6:8 (AV).

> This I say then, Walk in the Spirit, and ye shall not fulfill
> the lust of the flesh.

Galatians 5:16 (AV).

Muhammad's Revelation:

Alluring unto man is the enjoyment of worldly desires through women, and children, and heaped-up treasures of gold and silver, and horses of high mark, and cattle, and lands. All this may be enjoyed in the life of this world – But the most beauteous of all goals is with God.... For the God-conscious there are, with their Sustainer, gardens through which running waters flow, therein to abide, and spouses pure, and God's goodly acceptance.

The Qur'an. Āl-Imrān (The House of Imrān) 3:14–15.

... all who share in faith strive hard [in God's cause] with their possessions and their lives: and it is they whom the most excellent things await [in the life to come], and it is they, they who shall attain to a happy state! ... this is the triumph supreme!

The Qur'an. At-Tawbah (Repentance) 9:88–89.

Quakers:

Let all therefore mark well these three states and teachers; The God of truth was the first teacher, while man was in Paradise and in innocency. The serpent was the second teacher, the false teacher, who by his false teaching came to be the god of the world which lies in wickedness. Christ Jesus, that bruises the serpent's head is the third teacher, who says "Learn of me."

George Fox, *The Journal of George Fox*, "Speaking from Heaven," 1658. P. 313.

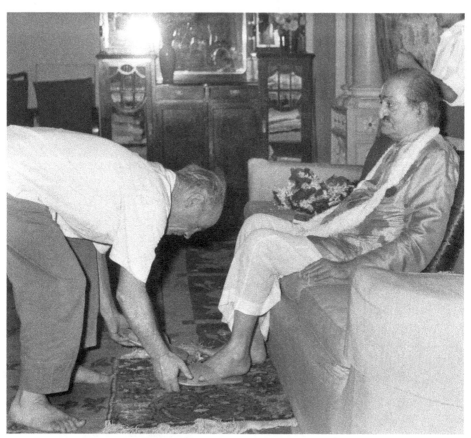

Francis Brabazon helping Avatar Meher Baba with his sandals, Guruprasad, Pune, India

PRINCIPLE 7

REAL SURRENDER IS RESIGNATION TO THE WILL OF GOD

7. The only Real Surrender is that in which poise is undisturbed by any adverse circumstance, and the individual, amidst every kind of hardship, is resigned with perfect calm to the will of God.

Meher Baba:

> Wanting is a state of disturbed equilibrium of mind, and nonwanting is a state of stable poise. The poise of nonwanting can only be maintained by an unceasing disentanglement from all stimuli—whether pleasant or painful, agreeable or disagreeable. In order to remain unmoved by the joys and sorrows of this world, the mind must be completely detached from the external and internal stimuli.

> Meher Baba, *Discourses*, revised 6th edition, vol. I, p. 68.

Zarathushtra:

> O Wise Follower of God, I have taught
> That action, not inaction, higher stands,
> Obeying, then, His Will, worship through deeds;
> The Great Lord, wondrous Guardian of the Worlds,

Through His Eternal Law discriminates,
Who are the truly Wise and who Unwise.
The Divine Songs of Zarathushtra. Ustavaiti 4.17
Yasna 46.17.

Krishna:

Surrendering all thoughts of outcome,
unperturbed, self-reliant,
he does nothing at all, even
when fully engaged in actions.

Bhagavad Gita. 4.20.

The resolute in yoga surrender
results, and gain perfect peace;
the irresolute, attached to results,
are bound by everything they do.

Bhagavad Gita. 5.12.

Tanakh:

When you pass through water,
I will be with you;
Through streams,
They shall not overwhelm you.
When you walk through fire,
You shall not be scorched;
Through flame,
It shall not burn you.
For I the Lord am your God,
The Holy One of Israel, your Savior.

Tanakh: The Holy Scriptures. Isaiah 43:2–3.

Buddha:

> Good people walk on, whatever befall; the good do not
> prattle, longing for pleasure; whether touched by
> happiness or sorrow, wise people never appear elated or
> depressed.

The Dhammapada. 6:83.

Jesus:

> "Not every one that saith unto me, Lord, Lord, shall enter
> into the kingdom of heaven; but he that doeth the will of
> my Father which is in heaven."

Matthew 7:21 (AV).

Muhammad's Revelation:

> O you who have attained to faith! Seek aid in steadfast
> patience and prayer: for, behold, God is with those who
> are patient in adversity…. And most certainly shall We
> try you by means of danger, and hunger, and loss of
> worldly goods, of lives and of [labour's] fruits. But give
> glad tidings unto those who are patient in adversity –
> who, when calamity befalls them, say, "Verily, unto God
> do we belong and, verily, unto Him we shall return."

The Qur'an. Al-Baqarah (The Cow) 2:153–156.

> "Hence, we shall certainly bear with patience whatever
> hurt you may do us: for, all who have trust [in His
> existence] must place their trust in God [alone]!"

The Qur'an. Ibrahim (Abraham) 14:12.

Quakers:

This people [Quakers] insists that Chrisitianity teaches
people to beat their swords into plowshares and their
spears into pruning hooks and never again to train for
war. They not only refused to take revenge for injuries
received, condemning it as unchristian, but they freely
forgave those who had been cruel to them—even when
vengeance was within their power. Many notable
examples of their efforts to overcome injustice and
oppression could be provided.

William Penn, *Twenty-First Century Penn: Writings on the Faith
and Practice of the People Called Quakers*, 1694. (Richmond,
Indiana: Earlham School of Religion Press, 2003), p. 364.

Meher Baba signing front pages of *God Speaks*, Satara, India, March 18, 1955

SECTION TWO

PROPER PURPOSE

Meher Baba at Guruprasad, Pune, India, November 1962

PRINCIPLE 8

LOVE IS EMPATHY

8. To love God in the most practical way is to love our fellow beings. If we feel for others in the same way as we feel for our own dear ones, we love God.

<u>Meher Baba:</u>

> Love is essentially self-communicative; those who do not have it catch it from those who have it. Those who receive love from others cannot be its recipients without giving a response that, in itself, is the nature of love. True love is unconquerable and irresistible. It goes on gathering power and spreading itself until eventually it transforms everyone it touches.
>
> Meher Baba, *Discourses*, revised 6th edition, vol. I, pp. 11-12.
>
> The dawn of love facilitates the death of selfishness.
>
> Meher Baba, *Discourses*, revised 6th edition, vol. I, p. 17

<u>Zarathushtra:</u>

> Whoso unto the Righteous acteth just,—
> Whether as 'Self-Reliant' he be known,
> Whether 'Co-worker' named, or 'Friend' addressed,—
> And whoso fosters zealously all Life,

He doth assure himself a place within
The Realm of Knowledge and of Love.

The Divine Songs of Zarathushtra. Ahunavaiti 6.3—Yasna
33.3.

Krishna:

He looks impartially on all:
those who love him or hate him,
his kinsmen, his enemies, his friends,
the good, and also the wicked.

Bhagavad Gita. 6.9.

He who has let go of hatred,
who treats all beings with kindness
and compassion, who is always serene,
unmoved by pain or pleasure,

free of the "I" and "mine,"
self-controlled, firm and patient,
his whole mind focused on me—
that man is the one I love best.

Bhagavad Gita. 12.13–14.

Tanakh:

Do not withhold good from one who deserves it
When you have the power to do it [for him].

Tanakh: The Holy Scriptures. Proverbs 3:27.

Buddha:

> If you examine this precious mind or emotion of
> altruism, of compassion, you will see that you need an
> object to generate even this feeling. And that object is a
> fellow human being. From this point of view, that very
> precious state of mind, compassion, is impossible
> without the presence of others....When you think along
> such lines, you will find sufficient grounds to feel
> connected with others, to feel the need to repay their
> kindness.

His Holiness the Dalai Lama; Robert Kiely, ed., *The Good
Heart: a Buddhist Perspective on the Teachings of Jesus.*
(Somerville, MA: Wisdom Publications, 1998
[paperback]), p. 68.

> In light of these convictions, it becomes impossible to
> believe that some people are totally irrelevant to your life
> or that you can afford to adopt an indifferent attitude
> toward them. There are no human beings that are
> irrelevant to your life.

The Good Heart. P. 68.

Jesus:

> Owe no man any thing, but to love one another: for he
> that loveth another hath fulfilled the law. For this, Thou
> shalt not commit adultery, Thou shalt not kill, Thou shalt
> not steal, Thou shalt not bear false witness, Thou shalt
> not covet; and if there be any other commandment, it is
> briefly comprehended in this saying, namely, Thou shalt
> love thy neighbour as thyself. Love worketh no ill to his
> neighbour: therefore love is the fulfilling of the law.

Romans 13:8–10 (AV).
<u>Muhammad's Revelation:</u>

> True piety does not consist in turning your faces towards
> the east or the west – but truly pious is he who believes
> in God ... and spends his substance – however much he
> himself may cherish it – upon his near of kin, and the
> orphans, and the needy, and the wayfarer, and the
> beggars, and for the freeing of human beings from
> bondage.

The Qur'an. Al-Baqarah (The Cow) 2:177.

<u>Quakers:</u>

> And all you that preach the truth, do it as it is in Jesus, in
> Love; He calls brethren; and He gives them power to
> become the sons of God and He gives them water of
> life; which shall be a well in them springing up as a river
> to eternal life. They may then water the spiritual plants
> of the living God. So that all might be spiritual planters,
> and spiritual waterers; so all might see with the spiritual
> eye the everlasting eternal God who is the eternal
> fountain.

George Fox, *The Journal of George Fox*, "Letter to Ford
Green," 1690. P. 346.

Meher Baba in seclusion, Cage Room, Upper Meherabad, India, July 30, 1941

PRINCIPLE 9

LOVE IS TAKING RESPONSIBILITY

9. If, instead of seeing faults in others, we look within ourselves, we are loving God.

Meher Baba:

> … When a person avoids backbiting and thinks more of the good points in others than of their bad points, and when he can practice supreme tolerance and desires the good of others even at the cost of his own self—he is ready to receive the grace of the Master.

Meher Baba, *Discourses*, revised 6th edition, vol. I, p. 166.

Zarathushtra:

> The strong wise man, guided by Law Divine,
> Or by his human heart, kindly receives
> All suppliants who come, though they be False;
> > He follows Knowledge's Path, he lives for Truth,
> > Their erring steps from soul destroying ways
> > To Self-reliance wisely shall he guide.

The Divine Songs of Zarathushtra. Ustavaiti 4.5—Yasna 46.5.

Krishna:

Fearlessness, purity of heart,
persistence in the yoga of knowledge,
generosity, self-control,
nonviolence, gentleness, candor ...

these are the qualities of men
born with divine traits, Arjuna.

Bhagavad Gita. 16.1, 3.

Tanakh:

He who seeks love overlooks faults,
But he who harps on a matter alienates his friend.
A rebuke works on an intelligent man
More than one hundred blows on a fool.

Tanakh: The Holy Scriptures. Proverbs 17:9–10.

You shall not take vengeance or bear a grudge against
your countrymen. Love your fellow as yourself: I am the
Lord.

Tanakh: The Holy Scriptures. Leviticus 19:18.

Buddha:

Not the perversities of others, not what they have done
or left undone should a sage take notice of.

The Dhammapada. 4:50.

The fault of others is easily perceived, but that of one's
self is difficult to perceive; a man winnows his
neighbours' faults like chaff, but hides his own, even as a
dishonest gambler hides a losing throw.

The Dhammapada. 18:252.

Jesus:

"Judge not that ye be not judged. For with what judgment
ye judge, ye shall be judged: and with what measure ye
mete, it shall be measured to you again. And why
beholdest thou the mote that is in thy brother's eye, but
considerest not the beam that is in thine own eye? ... first
cast out the beam out of thine own eye; and then shalt
thou see clearly to cast out the mote out of thy brother's
eye."

Matthew 7:1–5 (AV).

Muhammad's Revelation:

And never concern thyself with anything of which thou
hast no knowledge: verily, [thy] hearing and sight and
heart – all of them – will be called to account for it [on
Judgment Day]!

The Qur'an. Al-Isrãa (The Night Journey) 17:36.

Now those people have passed away; unto them shall be accounted what they have earned, and unto you, what you have earned; and you will not be judged on the strength of what they did.

The Qur'an. Al-Baqarah (The Cow) 2:141.

Quakers:

The priest said there might be a perfection as Adam had, certainly a falling from it. But I told him, "There is a perfection in Christ, above Adam and beyond falling; and that it was the work of the ministers of Christ to present every man perfect in Christ. Therefore those that denied perfection denied the work of the ministry." The priest said, "We must always be striving." But I told him it was a sad and comfortless way of striving, to strive with a belief that we should never overcome.

George Fox, *The Journal of George Fox*, "Declaration of Loyalty," 1660. P. 327.

St. Francis, by Cimabue,1278-80.
Basilica di San Francesco, Assisi, Italy

PRINCIPLE 10

LOVE IS GIVING TO OTHERS

10. If, instead of robbing others to help ourselves, we rob ourselves to help others, we are loving God.

<u>Meher Baba:</u>

> When a man realises that he can have a more glorious satisfaction by widening the sphere of his interests and activities, he is heading towards the life of service. At this stage he entertains many good desires. He wants to make others happy by relieving distress and helping them.

Meher Baba, *Discourses*, revised 6th edition, vol. I, p. 17

> ...As man entertains good desires his selfishness embraces a larger conception which eventually brings about its own extinction. Instead of merely trying to be luminous, arrestive, and possessive, man learns to be useful to others.

Meher Baba, *Discourses*, revised 6th edition, vol. I, p. 17

Zarathushtra:

As Lords Temporal work their will on Earth,
So by their gathered Knowledge Teachers wise;
The gifts of Love come as reward
For deeds done out of Love for Lord of Life;
God's Righteousness surely cometh down
On him who serves with zeal his brothers meek.

The Divine Songs of Zarathushtra. "Ahuna-Vairya," p. 17
("Ahuna Vairya" is one of the three daily prayers
—"The Three Sacred Verses").

Krishna:

He who acts for my sake,
loving me, free of attachment,
with benevolence toward all beings,
will come to me in the end.

Bhagavad Gita. 11.55.

Charity given to the worthy,
without any expectations,
for the sake of the act itself—
this kind of charity is sattvic.

Bhagavad Gita. 17.20.

Tanakh:

One man gives generously and ends with more;
Another stints on doing the right thing and incurs a loss.
A generous person enjoys prosperity;
He who satisfies others shall himself be sated.
He who withholds grain earns the curses of the people,
But blessings are on the head of the one who dispenses
it.

Tanakh: The Holy Scriptures. Proverbs 11:24–26.

He who withholds what is due to the poor affronts his
Maker; He who shows pity for the needy honors Him.

Tanakh: The Holy Scriptures. Proverbs 14:31.

Buddha:

May I be a protector for the unprotected;
A guide for travelers on the way;
A boat, a raft, or a bridge
For those who long to cross to the other shore.

May I be an isle for those who seek an island;
A lamp for those who wish for light;
A shelter for those in need of rest;
A servant for those in need of service.

Shantideva Bodhicaryavatara 3:17–18, as quoted in: His
Holiness the Dalai Lama, *Toward a True Kinship of Faiths*
(New York, NY: Three Rivers Press, 2010), p. 61.

Jesus:

> Hereby perceive we the love of God, because he laid down his life for us: and we ought to lay down our lives for the brethren. But whoso hath this world's good, and seeth his brother have need, and shutteth up his bowels of compassion from him, how dwelleth the love of God in him?

1 John 3:16–17 (AV).

Muhammad's Revelation:

> Be not, then, among the doubters: for, every community faces a direction of its own, of which He is the focal point. Vie, therefore, with one another in doing good works. Wherever you may be, God will gather you all unto Himself: for, verily, God has the power to will anything.

The Qur'an. Al-Baqarah (The Cow) 2:147–148.

> Yea, indeed: everyone who surrenders his whole being unto God, and is a doer of good withal, shall have his reward with his Sustainer; and all such need have no fear, and neither shall they grieve.

The Qur'an. Al-Baqarah (The Cow) 2:112.

Quakers:

> Therefore stir up the gift of God in you and improve it;
> do not sit down. Be valiant for God's Truth upon this
> earth. Go on in the Spirit, plowing with it and threshing
> with the power and Spirit of God, the wheat from the
> chaff of corruption. For he who looks back from the
> spiritual plow into the world is not likely to press into the
> life as the faithful do.

George Fox, *The Journal of George Fox*, "Letter to Edward
Mann," 1690. P. 268.

Meher Baba with Shariat Khan (third-plane *mast*), Bangalore, India, 1940

PRINCIPLE 11

LOVE IS COMPASSION

11. If we suffer in the suffering of others and feel happy in the happiness of others, we are loving God.

Meher Baba:

> The heart, which in its own way feels the unity of life, wants to fulfill itself through a life of love, sacrifice, and service. It is keen about giving instead of taking. It derives its driving power from the inmost psychic urge, expressing itself through the immediate intuitions of the inner life ... the heart, feeling in its inner experiences the glow of love, has glimpses of the unity of the spirit and therefore seeks expression through self-giving tendencies which unite man with man and makes him selfless and generous.

> Meher Baba, *Discourses*, revised 6th edition, vol. I, pp. 137-38.

Zarathushtra:

> To their Exalted Home shall I, indeed,
>   Lead Souls attuned to Love's Love :
> Being aware of blessings pouring down
>   On deeds performed in God's Name
> As long as I have will and wield the power
>   I'll teach mankind to love and strive for Truth.

> *The Divine Songs of Zarathush*tra. Ahunavaiti 2.4,Yasna 28.4

Krishna:

> When he sees all beings as equal
> in suffering or in joy
> because they are like himself,
> that man has grown perfect in yoga.

Bhagavad Gita. 6.32.

Tanakh:

> Learn to do good.
> Devote yourself to justice;
> Aid the wronged.
> Uphold the rights of the orphan;
> Defend the cause of the widow.

Tanakh: The Holy Scriptures. Isaiah 1:17.

Buddha:

> When a disciple is moved to make objective gifts of
> charity, he should also practice the Sila Paramita of
> selfless kindness, that is, he should remember that there is
> no arbitrary distinction between one's own self and the
> selfhood of others and, therefore, he should practice
> charity by giving, not objective gifts alone, but the selfless
> gifts of kindness and sympathy.

A Buddhist Bible. P. 91.

Good people walk on, whatever befall; the good do not prattle, longing for pleasure; whether touched by happiness or sorrow, wise people never appear elated or depressed.

The Dhammapada. 6:83.

Jesus:

Bear one another's burdens, and so fulfill the law of Christ.

Galatians 6:2 (AV).

If one member suffers, all suffer together; if one member is honored, all rejoice together.

1 Corinthians 12:26 (AV).

Muhammad's Revelation:

True piety does not consist in turning your faces towards the east or the west – but truly pious is he who believes in God ... and spends his substance – however much he himself may cherish it – upon his near of kin, and the orphans, and the needy, and the wayfarer, and the beggars, and for the freeing of human beings from bondage.

The Qur'an. Al-Baqarah (The Cow) 2:177.

The parable of those who spend their possessions for the sake of God is that of a grain out of which grow seven ears, in every ear a hundred grains: for God grants manifold increase unto whom He wills; and God is infinite, all-knowing. They who spend their possessions for the sake of God and do not thereafter mar their spending by stressing their own benevolence and hurting [the feelings of the needy] shall have their reward with their Sustainer, and no fear need they have, and neither shall they grieve. A kind word and the veiling of another's want is better than a charitable deed followed by hurt.

The Qur'an. Al-Baqarah (The Cow) 2:261–263.

Quakers:

I cried to the Lord saying, "Why should I be thus, seeing I was never addicted to commit these evils?" and the Lord answered that it was needful that I have a sense of all conditions, and in this I saw the infinite Love of God. I also saw that there was an ocean of darkness and death, but an infinite ocean of Light and Love which flowed over the ocean of darkness. In that also, I saw the infinite love of God; and I had great openings.

George Fox, *The Journal of George Fox*, "An Ocean of Light and Love," 1649. P. 11.

Avatar Meher Baba washing the feet of the poor, Ahmednagar, India, 1954

PRINCIPLE 12

LOVE IS GRATITUDE

12. If, instead of worrying over our own misfortunes, we think ourselves more fortunate than many, many others, we are loving God.

Meher Baba:

> One of the greatest obstacles hindering this spiritual preparation of the aspirant is worry. When, with supreme effort, this obstacle of worry is overcome, a way is paved for the cultivation of the divine attributes which constitute the spiritual preparation of the disciple.

> Meher Baba, *Discourses*, revised 6th edition, vol. I, p. 166.

> Worry is the product of feverish imagination working under the stimulus of desires. It is a living through of sufferings which are mostly our own creation. Worry has never done anyone any good; and it is very much worse than mere dissipation of psychic energy, for it substantially curtails the joy and fullness of life.

> Meher Baba, *Discourses*, revised 6th edition, vol. III, p. 125.

Zarathushtra:

One who always thinks of his own safety and profit, how can he love the joy-bringing Mother Earth? The righteous man that follows Knowledge's Law shall dwell in regions radiant with Thy Sun, the abode where wise ones dwell.

Mobed Firouz 'Azargoshasb, *Translation of Gathas: The Holy Songs Of Zarathushtra*. (2017: https:// www.zarathushtra.com). Yasna 50, Verse 2.

How shall one woo joy-bringing Mother Earth,
While thinking thoughts of his own selfish gains?
The Righteous man, that follows Knowledge's Law,
Shall dwell in regions radiant with Thy Sun,
His place shall be in Wisdom's own Abode.

The Divine Songs of Zarathushtra. Spenta-Mainyu 4.2— Yasna 50.2.

Krishna:

[Wise men] do not rejoice in good fortune;
they do not lament at bad fortune;
lucid, with minds unshaken,
they remain within what is real.

Bhagavad Gita. 5.20.

The wise man, cleansed of his sins,
who has cut off all separation,
who delights in the welfare of all beings,
vanishes into God's bliss.

Bhagavad Gita. 5.25.

<u>Tanakh:</u>

Many say, "O for good days!"
Bestow Your favor on us, O Lord.
You put joy into my heart
    when their grain and wine show increase.
Safe and sound, I lie down and sleep,
    for You alone, O Lord, keep me secure.

Tanakh: The Holy Scriptures. Psalms 4:7–9.

<u>Buddha:</u>

Let him not disdain what he has received, let him not
envy others; a monk who envies others does not attain
(the tranquility of) meditation.

The Dhammapada. 25:365.

<u>Jesus:</u>

Jesus looked up and saw the rich putting their gifts into
the offering box, and he saw a poor widow put in two
small copper coins. And he said, "Truly, I tell you, this
poor widow has put in more than all of them. For they all
contributed out of their abundance, but she out of her
poverty put in all she had to live on."

Luke 21:1–4 (AV).

Muhammad's Revelation:

Guide us in the straight way – the way of those upon whom Thou hast bestowed Thy blessings, not of those who have been condemned [by Thee], nor of those who go astray.

The Qur'an. Al-Fatihah (The Opening) 1:6–7.

Quakers:

Not all people receive and obey the Light within. All have the ability to reason, but not all are reasonable. Is it the fault of the grain stored in the granary that it does not grow; or of money hidden in a napkin that it does not earn interest? So, if those who object will tell us whose fault it is that some have wasted their gift, we are prepared to tell them why the unprofitable servant was not rewarded. The blind must not blame the sun for their blindness, nor should sinners accuse Grace of being inadequate.

William Penn, *Twenty-First Century Penn*, "Primitive Chrisitianity Revived," 1696. P. 301.

Sa'ghi bi'ya ke ha'te'fe ghey'bam be mozh'de goft
Ba dard sabr kon, ke da'va mi'fe'res'ta'mat.

Saki! Come; for the invisible messenger uttered
to me glad tidings,
"In pain, exercise patience; for the remedy of
Union I send Thee."

Hafiz

PRINCIPLE 13

LOVE IS PATIENCE
AND CONTENTMENT

13. If we endure our lot with patience and contentment, accepting it as His Will, we are loving God.

Meher Baba:

> … One of the first requirements of the aspirant is that he should combine unfailing enthusiasm with unyielding patience. Once a man is determined to realise the Truth, he finds that his Path is beset with many difficulties, and there are very few who persist with steady courage till the very end. It is easy to give up the effort when one is confronted with obstacles.

> Meher Baba, *Discourses*, revised 6th edition, vol. III, pp. 121-22.

> If man becomes desireless and contented, he will be free from his self-inflicted suffering. His imagination will not be constantly harassed by feverish reaching out toward things that really do not matter, and he will be established in unassailable peace. When man is thus contented, he does not require any solutions to problems, because the problems which confront worldly persons have disappeared. He has no problems, therefore he does not have to worry about their solution. For him the complexities of life do not exist because his life becomes utterly simple in the state of desirelessness.

Meher Baba, *Discourses*, revised 6th edition, vol. III, p. 176.

Zarathushtra:

That I the better way might choose, reveal,
    What in accord with Truth Thou hast ordained;
Reveal to me through Love, through Love,
    That I might be uplifted and be sure,
Whatever comes at Thy Command is best
    For me—whether reward or otherwise.

The Divine Songs of Zarathushtra. Ahunavaiti 4.5—Yasna 31.5.

Krishna:

When a man gives up all desires
that emerge from the mind, and rests
contented in the Self by the Self,
he is called a man of firm wisdom.

Bhagavad Gita. 2.55.

Tanakh:

Then Job arose, tore his robe, cut off his hair, and threw himself on the ground and worshiped. He said, "Naked came I out of my mother's womb, and naked shall I return there; the Lord has given, and the Lord has taken away; blessed be the name of the Lord."

Tanakh: The Holy Scriptures. Job 1:20.

Buddha:

Patience, long-suffering, is the highest form of penance,
Nirvana the highest of all things, say the Awakened; for
he is not an anchorite who strikes another, he is not an
ascetic who insults another.

The Dhammapada. 14:184.

Jesus:

Cast not away therefore your confidence, which hath
great recompense of reward. For ye have need of
patience, that, after ye have done the will of God, ye
might receive the promise.

Hebrews 10:35–36 (AV).

Muhammad's Revelation:

Verily, in this [reminder] there are messages indeed for all
who are wholly patient in adversity and deeply grateful [to
God].

The Qur'an. Ibrahim (Abraham) 14:5.

Clearly, indeed, have We spelled out these messages unto
people who [are willing to] take them to heart! Theirs
shall be an abode of peace with their Sustainer; and He
shall be near unto them in result of what they have been
doing.

The Qur'an. Al-Anãm (Cattle) 6:126–127.

Quakers:

We must have patience for should the first lesson contain everything? Students who are willing to learn and who listen to and follow the directions of a capable teacher will grow in knowledge. If they do not attend to the master, their failure to learn should be laid at their feet, not the teachers. Consider this from the gospel of John: "if you do my will, you will learn more of my doctrine."

William Penn, *Twenty-First Century Penn*, "The Christian Quaker," 1674. P. 98.

Meher Baba, 1939

PRINCIPLE 14

LOVE IS DOING
NO HARM

14. If we understand and feel that the greatest act of devotion and worship to God is not to hurt or harm any of His beings, we are loving God.

Meher Baba:

> Nonviolence pure and simple means Love Infinite. It is the goal of life. When this state of pure and Infinite Love is reached, the aspirant is at one with God. To reach this goal there must be intense longing, and the aspirant who has this longing to realise the supreme state has to begin by practising what is termed "nonviolence of the brave." This applies to those who, though not one with all through actual realisation, consider no one as their enemy. They try to win over even the aggressor through love and give up their lives by being attacked, not through fear but through love.

> Meher Baba, *Discourses*, revised 6th edition, vol. I, pp. 107-08.

Zarathushtra:

> Keep Hatred far from you; let nothing tempt
> Your minds to violence:—hold on to Love.

The Divine Songs of Zarathushtra. Spenta-Mainyu 2.7—
Yasna 48.7.

Krishna:

> Knowing that it is eternal,
> unborn, beyond destruction,
> how could you ever kill?
> And whom could you kill, Arjuna?

Bhagavad Gita. 2.21.

> He who neither disturbs
> the world nor is disturbed by it,
> who is free of all joy, fear, envy—
> that man is the one I love best.

Bhagavad Gita. 12.15.

Tanakh:

> Do not devise harm against your fellow
> Who lives trustfully with you.

Tanakh: The Holy Scriptures. Proverbs 3:29.

> The wolf and the lamb shall graze together,
> And the lion shall eat straw like the ox,
> And the serpent's food shall be earth.
> In all My sacred mount
> Nothing evil or vile shall be done
> —said the Lord.

Tanakh: The Holy Scriptures. Isaiah 65:25.

Buddha:

> He who, seeking his own happiness, does not injure or kill beings who also long for happiness, will find happiness after death.

The Dhammapada. 10:132.

> He who, though richly adorned, exercises tranquility, is quiet, subdued, restrained, chaste, and has ceased to injure all other beings, is indeed Brahman, an ascetic, a friar.

The Dhammapada. 10:142.

> What now is Right Action? There someone avoids the killing of living beings, and abstains from it. Without stick or sword, conscientious, full of sympathy, he is anxious for the welfare of all living beings.

A Buddhist Bible. P. 44.

Jesus:

> "But I say unto you, Love your enemies, bless them that curse you, do good to them that hate you, and pray for them which despitefully use you, and persecute you; That ye may be the children of your Father which is in heaven; for he maketh his sun to rise on the evil and on the good, and sendeth rain on the just and on the unjust."

Matthew 5:44–45 (AV).

Muhammad's Revelation:

And do not take any human being's life – [the life] which
God has willed to be sacred – otherwise than in [the
pursuit of] justice. Hence, if anyone has been slain
wrongfully, We have empowered the defender of his
rights [to exact a just retribution]; but even so, let him not
exceed the bounds of equity in [retributive] killing. [And
as for him who has been slain wrongfully –] behold, he is
indeed succoured [by God]!

The Qur'an. Al-Israa (The Night Journey) 17:32–33.

Quakers:

They urge all to turn their zeal loose on sin and no longer
to make war against each other. All wars and fightings
arise in human covetousness not from the meek Spirit of
Christ Jesus. Christ is the captain of a different warfare
carried out with different weapons. Just as swearing gave
way to speaking Truth, fighting gave way to faith and
truth as Quaker doctrines and practices.

William Penn, Twenty-First Century Penn, "Rise and
Progress of the People Called Quakers," 1694. P. 365.

Joz as'ta'ne to'am dar ja;han pa'na'hi nist,
Sa're mas ra be joz in dar, ha've'le ga'hi nist.

Save thy threshold, my shelter in the world is none,
Save this door, my fortress-place is none.

Hafiz

PRINCIPLE 15

LOVE IS LIVING
BY SPIRITUAL PRINCIPLES

15. To love God as He ought to be loved, we must live for God and die for God, knowing that the goal of life is to love God, and find Him as our own Self.

Meher Baba:

> God is worth living for, and He is also worth dying for. All else is a vain and empty pursuit of illusory values.

> Meher Baba, *Discourses*, revised 6th edition, vol. III, p. 100.

> Divine love is unlimited in essence and expression because it is experienced by the soul through the Soul itself. ... Divine love is entirely free from the thralldom of desires or the limiting self. In this state of Infinity the lover has no being apart from the Beloved: he is the Beloved Himself.

> Meher Baba, *Discourses*, revised 6th edition, vol. III, p. 188.

Zarathushtra:

He, through His Holy Word, did first declare,
His LIGHT shall stream through all the Lights on high;
Himself, All-Wise, the Law of Truth declared,
That this His LIGHT might glow as LOVE Supreme;—
Make it blaze higher, God, through the grace
Of Thine own Spirit, evermore the same.

The Divine Songs of Zarathushtra. Ahunavaiti 4.7—Yasna
31.7.

Thus may I realise Thee as the First
And also Last, O God, in my mind,
As Father of all LOVE—of Love;
Thus may I ever hold Thee in mine eye,
As the true Parent of ETERNAL LAW,
As Judge Supreme of every act of man.

The Divine Songs of Zarathushtra. Ahunavaiti 4.8— Yasna
31.8.

Krishna:

Concentrate your mind on me,
fill your heart with my presence,
love me, serve me, worship me,
and you will attain me at last.

Bhagavad Gita. 9.34.

Whatever you do, Arjuna,
do it as an offering to me—

whatever you say or eat
or pray or enjoy or suffer.

Bhagavad Gita. 9.27.

Tanakh:

You shall love the Lord your God with all your heart and
with all your soul and with all your might.

Tanakh: The Holy Scriptures. Deuteronomy 6:5.

But be very careful to fulfill the Instruction and the
Teaching that Moses the servant of the Lord enjoined
upon you, to love the Lord your God and to walk in all
His ways, and to keep His commandments and hold fast
to Him, and to serve Him with all your heart and soul.

Tanakh: The Holy Scriptures. Joshua 22:5.

Buddha:

Hence, the purpose of the Holy Life does not consist in
acquiring alms, honour, or fame, nor in gaining morality,
concentration, or the eye of knowledge. That unshakable
deliverance of the heart: that, verily, is the object of the
Holy Life, that is the essence, that is the goal.

A Buddhist Bible. P. 59–60.

Jesus:

But if any man love God, the same is known of him.

1 Corinthians 8:3 (AV).

Beloved, let us love one another: for love is of God; and every one that loveth is born of God, and knoweth God. He that loveth not knoweth not God; for God is love.

1 John 4:7–8 (AV).

Muhammad's Revelation:

God is near unto those who have faith, taking them out of deep darkness into the light – whereas near unto those who are bent on denying the truth are the powers of evil that take them out of the light into darkness deep.

The Qur'an. Al-Baqarah (The Cow) 2:257.

"… Behold, it shall be a sign of his [rightful] dominion that you will be granted a heart endowed by your Sustainer with inner peace and with all that is enduring."

The Qur'an. Al-Baqarah (The Cow) 2:248.

Quakers:

In the power of life and wisdom, and dread of the Lord God of life, and heaven, and earth, dwell in the wisdom of God that over all may be preserved. Be a terror to the adversaries of God answering that of God in them all, spreading the Truth abroad, awakening the witness, confounding deceit. Let all nations hear the sound by word or writing. Spare no place, spare no tongue nor pen; but be obedient to the Lord God.

George Fox, *The Journal of George Fox*, "Jailer Becomes Prisoner," 1651. P. 134.

Meher Baba on a picnic, Trimbak, India, March 25, 1937

SECTION THREE

PROPER EFFORT

"Rush to Your Feet to Work"

ی می زنی کار پا بشد زدست رگ

د، هم نوایی می زن ر پای نمانو

گر نیست تو را ، بعقل رأیی می زن

حاصل، هر دم، دم وفایی می زن

Gar dast beshod ze kar payie mizan,

Var payee na monad ham navaee mizan,

Gar nist tora beagl rayee mizan,

Hasel hardam dameh vafayie mizan.

If your hand has stopped working, rush to your feet to work,

And if your feet stop working then strike up a song as well,

If there is nothing for you to do, consult with your reason,

In any case, with each breath be faithful to the Beloved every moment.

Maulana Rumi

Translation by Mehernoush McPherson and Tom Wolfe

PRINCIPLE 16

DO NOT SHIRK
YOUR RESPONSIBILITIES

16. The lover has to keep the wish of the Beloved. My wish for my lovers is as follows: Do not shirk your responsibilities.

Meher Baba:

> Real spiritual experience involves not only realisation of the nature of the soul while on higher planes of consciousness but also a right attitude towards worldly duties. If it loses its connection with the different phases of life, what we have is a neurotic reaction that is far from being a spiritual experience.

> Meher Baba, *Discourses*, revised 6th edition, vol. I, pp. 7-8

Zarathushtra:

> O Wise Follower of God, I have taught
> That action, not inaction, higher stands,
> Obeying, then, His Will, worship through deeds;
> The Great Lord, wondrous Guardian of the Worlds,
> Through His Eternal Law discriminates,
> Who are the truly Wise and who Unwise.

> *The Divine Songs of Zarathushtra*. Ustavaiti 4.17—Yasna 46.17.

Krishna:

Know what your duty is
and do it without hesitation.
For a warrior, there is nothing better
than a battle that duty enjoins.

Bhagavad Gita. 2.31.

Without concern for results,
perform the necessary action;
surrendering all attachments,
accomplish life's highest good.

Bhagavad Gita. 3.19.

Tanakh:

You represent the people before God: you bring the
disputes before God, and enjoin upon them the laws and
the teachings, and make known to them the way they are
to go and the practices they are to follow.

Tanakh: The Holy Scriptures. Exodus 18:19–20.

Six days you shall labor and do all your work.

Tanakh: The Holy Scriptures. Exodus 20:9.

Buddha:

> He who possesses character and discrimination, who is just, speaks the truth, and does what is his own business, him the world will hold dear.

> *The Dhammapada.* 16:217.

Jesus:

> But this I say, He which soweth sparingly shall reap also sparingly; and he which soweth bountifully shall reap also bountifully. Every man according as he purposeth in his heart, so let him give; not grudgingly, or of necessity: for God loveth a cheerful giver. And God is able to make all grace abound toward you; that ye, always having all sufficiency in all things, may abound to every good work.

> 2 Corinthians 9:6–8 (AV).

Muhammad's Revelation:

> And give full measure whenever you measure, and weigh with a balance that is true: this will be [for your own] good, and best in the end.

> *The Qur'an.* Al-Israa (The Night Journey) 17:35.

> O you who have attained to faith! Seek aid in steadfast patience and prayer: for, behold, God is with those who are patient in adversity.

> *The Qur'an.* Al-Baqarah (The Cow) 2:153.

Quakers:

While Jesus relieved the sufferings of his fellow beings, he at the same time infused his blessed gospel of glad tidings of great joy unto all people, by directing them to that fount within themselves, whence the pure water which springs up into everlasting life—that heavenly manna which all might partake of—that which comes down from heaven, from a source higher than earth, and nourishes the immortal soul. He then never separated his spiritual from his outward duties.

Lucretia Mott, *Lucretia Mott Speaks*, "Sermon at Cherry Street Meeting, Mercy and Love" 1850. P. 85.

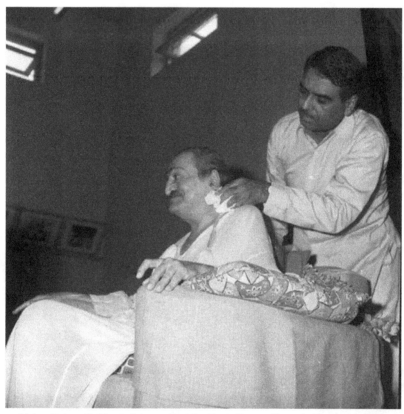

Meher Baba with Eruch Jessawala at the Pune Center, Pune, India, May 1, 1965

PRINCIPLE 17

ATTEND TO YOUR DUTIES BUT DO NOT BE ATTACHED TO RESULTS

17. Attend faithfully to your worldly duties, but keep always at the back of your mind that all this is Baba's.

Meher Baba:

> Spirituality does not require the external renunciation of worldly activities or the avoiding of duties and responsibilities. It only requires that, while performing the worldly activities or discharging the responsibilities arising from the specific place and position of the individual, the inner spirit should remain free from the burden of desires.

> Meher Baba, *Discourses*, revised 6th edition, vol. I, p. 20.

Zarathushtra:

> The path, O God, which Thou hast shown me is the path of Love, the path based on the teachings of Saoshyants, the saviors. The teaching which recommends that the work performed with the view of performing one's duty honestly shall bring forth happiness. The teaching which leads mankind to real knowledge and wisdom, and reaching Thee O God, is its rewards.

Translation of Gathas: The Holy Songs Of Zarathushtra. Yasna 34, Verse 13.

The Path, O God, of Love,
That One Path hast Thou pointed out to me, —
The ancient Teaching of all Saviours,—
That good deeds done for their own sake lead far:—
This Teaching leads mankind to Wisdom true,
That single Prize of Life—Thyself the Goal.

The Divine Songs of Zarathushtra. Ahunavaiti 7.13— Yasna 34.13.

Krishna:

The whole world becomes a slave
to its own activity, Arjuna;
if you want to be truly free,
perform all actions as worship.

Bhagavad Gita. 3.9.

When a man sees clearly that there is
no doer besides the gunas
and knows what exists beyond them,
he can enter my state of being.

Bhagavad Gita. 14.19.

Tanakh:

What real value is there for a man
In all the gains he makes beneath the sun?

One generation goes, another comes,
But the earth remains the same forever.
The sun rises, and the sun sets—
And glides back to where it rises....
All such things are wearisome:
No man can ever state them;
The eye never has enough of seeing,
Nor the ear enough of hearing.
Only that shall happen
Which has happened,
Only that occur
Which has occurred;
There is nothing new
Beneath the sun!

Tanakh: The Holy Scriptures. Ecclesiastes 1:3–5, 8–9.

Buddha:

Such a man who does his duty is tolerant like the earth,
like a stone set in a threshold; he is like a lake without
mud; no new births are in store for him.

The Dhammapada. 7:95.

Jesus:

"But lay up for yourselves treasures in heaven, where
neither moth nor rust doth corrupt, and where thieves do
not break through nor steal: For where your treasure is,
there will your heart be also."

Matthew 6:20–21 (AV).

"Let your light so shine before men, that they may see your good works, and glorify your Father which is in heaven."

Matthew 5:16 (AV).

Muhammad's Revelation:

But woe unto those who deny the truth: for suffering severe awaits those who choose the life of this world as the sole object of their love, preferring it to [all thought of] the life to come, and who turn others away from the path of God and try to make it appear crooked. Such as these have indeed gone far astray!

The Qur'an. Ibrahim (Abraham) 14:2–3.

… people whom neither [worldly] commerce nor striving after gain can divert from the remembrance of God.

The Qur'an. An-Nur (The Light) 24:37.

Quakers:

If there is any one thing more strongly inculcated in the testimony of the ancients it is the duty of administering to the necessities of the suffering, of giving aid to the weak and perishing. Righteous conduct, right doing, good works, practical righteousness, or whatever name we apply to it, has been inculcated by the good—the truly pious in all ages of the world.

Lucretia Mott, *Lucretia Mott Speaks*, "Sermon at Cherry Street Meeting, Mercy and Love," 1850. P. 85.

Meher Baba, ca. 1940, Bangalore, India

PRINCIPLE 18

ACCEPT HAPPINESS AND SUFFERING WITH EQUAL POISE

18. When you feel happy, think: "Baba wants me to be happy." When you suffer, think: "Baba wants me to suffer."

Meher Baba:

> It is your right to be happy, and yet you create your own unhappiness by wanting things. Wanting is the source of perpetual restlessness. If you do not get the thing you wanted, you are disappointed. And if you get it, you want more and more of it and become unhappy. Say "I do not want anything" and be happy. The continuous realisation of the futility of wants will eventually lead you to Knowledge. This Self-knowledge will give you the freedom from wants which leads to the road to abiding happiness.

Meher Baba, *Discourses*, revised 6th edition, vol. I, p. 16

Serving the Master is a joy for the disciple, even when it means an ordeal that tries his body or mind. Service offered under conditions of discomfort or inconvenience is a test of the disciple's devotion. The more trying such service becomes, the more welcome it is for the disciple, and as he voluntarily accepts physical and mental suffer

ing in his devoted service to the Master, he experiences
the bliss of spiritual fulfillment.

Meher Baba, *Discourses*, revised 6th edition, vol. II, p. 42

Zarathushtra:

> I ask, God, that I learn from Thee,
>   How Fate has come upon us, and shall come;
> What silent yearnings of good men and true
>   Have been recorded in the Book of Life,
> What yearnings, too, that follow the Untruth;
>   How do these stand, when the account is closed?

The Divine Songs of Zarathushtra. Ahunavaiti 4.14—Yasna
31.14.

Krishna:

> He whose mind is untroubled
> by any misfortune, whose craving
> for pleasures has disappeared,
> who is free from greed, fear, anger,
>
> who is unattached to all things,
> who neither grieves nor rejoices
> if good or if bad things happen—
> that man is a man of firm wisdom.

Bhagavad Gita. 2.56–57.

… quiet, filled with devotion,
content with whatever happens,
at home wherever he is—
that man is the one I love best.

Bhagavad Gita. 12.19.

Tanakh:

See how happy is the man whom God reproves;
Do not reject the discipline of the Almighty.
He injures, but He binds up;
He wounds, but His hands heal.
He will deliver you from six troubles;
In seven no harm will reach you:
In famine He will redeem you from death,
In war, from the sword.

Tanakh: The Holy Scriptures. Job 5:17–20.

Buddha:

Good people walk on, whatever befall; the good do not
prattle, longing for pleasure; whether touched by
happiness or sorrow, wise people never appear elated or
depressed.

The Dhammapada. 6:83.

Just as a rock of one solid mass remains unshaken by the wind, even so, neither forms, nor sounds, nor odours, nor tastes, nor contacts of any kind, neither the desired nor the undesired, can cause such an [*sic*] one to waver. Steadfast is his mind, gained is deliverance.

A Buddhist Bible. P. 32.

Jesus:

We are troubled on every side, yet not distressed; we are perplexed, but not in despair; Persecuted, but not forsaken; cast down, but not destroyed.

2 Corinthians 4:8–9 (AV).

But seek ye first the kingdom of God, and his righteousness; and all these things shall be added unto you. Take therefore no thought for the morrow; for the morrow shall take thought for the things of itself. Sufficient unto the day is the evil thereof."

Matthew 6:33–34 (AV).

Muhammad's Revelation:

And God endows those who avail themselves of [His] guidance with an ever-deeper consciousness of the right way; and good deeds, the fruit whereof endures forever, are, in thy Sustainer's sight, of far greater merit [than any worldly goods], and yield far better returns.

The Qur'an. Marayam (Mary) 19:76.

[But] do you think that you could enter paradise without having suffered like those [believers] who passed away before you? Misfortune and hardship befell them, and so shaken were they that the apostle, and the believers with him, would exclaim, "When will God's succor come?" Oh, verily, God's succour is [always] near!

The Qur'an. Al-Baqarah (The Cow) 2:214.

Quakers:

At times I turned to folly, and then sorrow and confusion took hold of me. Thus for some months I had great troubles; my will was unsubjected, which rendered my labors fruitless. At length, through the merciful continuance of heavenly visitations, I was made to bow down in spirit before the Lord. I must say in reverence, he was near to me in my troubles, and in those times of humiliation opened my ear to discipline.

John Woolman, Harvard Classics, *The Journal of John Woolman, 1721*. (New York, NY: P.F. Collier and Son Corporation, 1937), p. 172.

Gof'tam za'ma'ne esh'rat, di'di ke chun sar a'mad
Gof'ta kha'mush ha'fez kin ghos'se ham sar a'yad.

I said: "Thou sayest how quickly the time of ease
came to an end."
He said: "Hafiz! Silence. For to an end
this grief also will come."

Hafiz

PRINCIPLE 19

ACCEPT WHAT COMES WITHOUT RESENTMENT

19. Be resigned to every situation and think honestly and sincerely: "Baba has placed me in this situation."

Meher Baba:

> The self-surrender amounts to an open admission that the aspirant now has given up all hope of tackling the problems of the ego by himself and that he relies solely upon the Master.

> Meher Baba, *Discourses*, revised 6th edition, vol. II, p. 73.

> The shifting of interest from unimportant things to important values is facilitated by allegiance and self-surrender to the Master, who becomes the new nucleus for integration.

> Meher Baba, *Discourses*, revised 6th edition, vol. II, pp. 82-83.

Zarathushtra:

> Of all these sinners none doth understand
>   What true and lasting progress might imply,
> This can be learnt from Life on earth alone,—
>   The "test of molten brass" proclaimed by Thee;

The final end of sinners, God,
　　Were best, O God, judged by Thee alone.

The Divine Songs of Zarathushtra. Ahunavaiti 5.7—Yasna 32.7.

Krishna:

When a man has become unattached
to sense-objects or to actions,
renouncing his own selfish will,
then he is mature in yoga.

Bhagavad Gita. 6.4.

… detachment, absence of clinging
to son, wife, family, and home,
an unshakeable equanimity
in good fortune or in bad …

all this is called true knowledge;
what differs from it is called ignorance.

Bhagavad Gita. 13.9, 11.

Tanakh:

What value, then, can the man of affairs get from what he
earns? I have observed the business that God gave man
to be concerned with: He brings everything to pass
precisely at its time; He also puts eternity in their mind,
but without man ever guessing, from first to last, all the
things that God brings to pass. Thus I realized that the
only worthwhile thing there is for them is to enjoy
themselves and do what is good in their lifetime; also, that

whenever a man does eat and drink and get enjoyment out of all his wealth, it is a gift of God.

Tanakh: The Holy Scriptures. Ecclesiastes 3:9–13.

Buddha:

Patience, long-suffering, is the highest form of penance, Nirvana that highest of all things, say the Awakened.

The Dhammapada. 14:184.

Victory breeds hatred, for the conquered is unhappy. He who has given up both victory and defeat, he, the contented, is happy.

The Dhammapada. 15:201.

Jesus:

Likewise the Spirit also helpeth our infirmities: for we know not what we should pray for as we ought: but the Spirit itself maketh intercession for us with groanings which cannot be uttered.

Romans 8:26 (AV).

Muhammad's Revelation:

O you who have attained to faith! Seek aid in steadfast patience and prayer: for, behold, God is with those who are patient in adversity.

The Qur'an. Al-Baqarah (The Cow) 2:153.

Quakers:

And now, dear Friends, with respect to the commotions and stirrings of the earth at this time near us, we are desirous that none of us may be moved thereby, but repose ourselves in the munition of that rock which all these shakings shall not move. For the truth is but one, and many are the partakers of the spirit of it, so the world is but one.

John Woolman, *The Journal of John Woolman* (HC), 1775. P. 191.

Meher Baba feeding a *mast* at the ashram in Bangalore, India, 1939

PRINCIPLE 20

HELP AND SERVE OTHERS

20. With the understanding that Baba is in everyone, try to help and serve others.

Meher Baba:

> … In being useful to a co-aspirant in doing the Master's work, the aspirant is rendering a service to him as much as to the Master.

> Meher Baba, *Discourses*, revised 6th edition, vol. III, p.133.

> The life of the Master is a life of service; it is a perpetual offering to other forms of his own Self.

> Meher Baba, *Discourses*, revised 6th edition, vol. I, p. 135.

Zarathushtra:

> Such are, indeed, the Saviours of the Earth,
> They follow Duty's call, the call of Love :
> God, they listen unto Love;
>   They do what Knowledge bids, and Thy Commands;
>   Surely they are the Vanquishers of Hate.

> *The Divine Songs of Zarathushtra*. Spenta-Mainyu 2.12—
> Yasna 48.12.

Krishna:

The same to both friend and foe,
the same in disgrace or honor,
suffering or joy, untroubled,
indifferent to praise or blame ...
that man is the one I love best.

Bhagavad Gita. 12.18, 19.

Knowledge that sees in all things
a single, imperishable being,
undivided among the divided—
this kind of knowledge is sattvic.*

Bhagavad Gita. 18.20.

Tanakh:

You shall not take vengeance or bear a grudge against
your countrymen. Love your fellow as yourself: I am the
Lord.

Tanakh: The Holy Scriptures. Leviticus 19:18.

Buddha:

In like manner his good works receive him who has done
good, and has gone from this world to the other—as
kinsmen receive one who is dear to them on his return.

The Dhammapada. 16:220.

---

* Sattva is characterized as "pure"; in Hinduism, it represents the principle of pure thought.

The disciples of Gotama are always wide awake and watchful, and their mind day and night ever delights in compassion.

The Dhammapada. 21:300.

Jesus:

"But when thou makest a feast, call the poor, the maimed, the lame, the blind: And thou shalt be blessed; for they cannot recompense thee: for thou shalt be recompensed at the resurrection of the just."

Luke 14:13-14 (AV).

Muhammad's Revelation:

And neither allow thy hand to remain shackled to thy neck, nor stretch it forth to the utmost limit [of thy capacity], lest thou find thyself blamed [by thy dependents], or even destitute. Behold, thy Sustainer grants abundant sustenance, or gives it in scant measure, unto whomever He wills: verily, fully aware is He of [the needs of] His creatures, and sees them all.

The Qur'an. Al-Israa (The Night Journey) 17:29–30.

Quakers:

From an inward purifying, and steadfast abiding under it
springs a lively operative desire for the good of others.
The outward modes of worship are various; but
whenever any are true ministers of Jesus Christ, it is from
the operation of the Spirit upon their hearts, first
purifying them, and thus giving them a just sense of the
conditions of others.

John Woolman, *The Journal of John Woolman* (HC), 1779. P.
176.

Fek're bol'bol hame an ast ke gol shod ya'rash,
Del'e hafez ke be di'dar'e to khu'gar sh'de bud
Naz'par'var'de ve'sal ast ma'ju aza'rash.

The thought of the nightingale all is that,
that the rose, his beloved may be,
The heart of Hafiz has become so
accustomed to the sight of Thee
His heart is cherished with union, its torment, seek not.

Hafiz

PRINCIPLE 21

REMEMBER GOD WITH YOUR DYING BREATH

21. I say with my Divine Authority to each and all that whosoever takes my name at the time of breathing his last comes to me; so do not forget to remember me in your last moments. Unless you start remembering me from now on, it will be difficult to remember me when your end approaches. You should start practising from now on. Even if you take my name only once every day, you will not forget to remember me in your dying moments.

Meher Baba:

> Thus a person who is not very learned but who sincerely takes the name of God and does his humble duties wholeheartedly may actually be nearer to God than one who knows all the metaphysics of the world but who does not allow any of his theories to modify his everyday life.

Meher Baba, *Discourses*, revised 6th edition, vol. II, p. 205

Zarathushtra:

> And if some be, who in their Righteousness,
>   And by their Loving Hearts appear to Thee,
>   As truly-seeing and upright, O Lord,
> Grant them in full all that their Souls desire;

147

For I believe no prayer devout for Truth
Can ever remain unanswered from Your side.

The Divine Songs of Zarathushtra. Ahunavaiti 2.10—Yasna 28.10.

Krishna:

Whoever in his final moments
thinks of me only, is sure
to enter my state of being
once his body is dead.

Bhagavad Gita. 8.5.

If you do this at the hour of your death,
with an unmoving mind, drawing
your breath up between your eyebrows,
you will reach the Person that I am.

Bhagavad Gita. 8.10.

Tanakh:

But let all who take refuge in You rejoice,
    ever jubilant as You shelter them;
        and let those who love Your name exult in You.
For You surely bless the righteous man, O Lord,
    encompassing him with favor like a shield.

Tanakh: The Holy Scriptures. Psalms 5:12–13.

Buddha:

> He who takes refuge with Buddha, the Law and the
> Order; he who with clear understanding sees the four
> noble truths: –
> Suffering, the origin of suffering, the destruction of
> suffering, and the eightfold noble path that leads to the
> release from suffering –
> That is the safe refuge, that is the best refuge; having
> gone to that refuge, a man is delivered from all suffering.

The Dhammapada. 14:190–192.

Jesus:

> "Therefore whosoever heareth these sayings of mine, and
> doeth them, I will liken him unto a wise man, which built
> his house upon a rock: And the rain descended, and the
> floods came, and the winds blew, and beat upon that
> house; and it fell not: for it was founded upon a rock."

Matthew 7:24–25 (AV).

Muhammad's Revelation:

> Say: "Invoke God, or invoke the Most Gracious: by
> whichever name you invoke Him, [He is always the One –
> for] His are all the attributes of perfection."

The Qur'an. Al-Israa (The Night Journey) 17:110.

"Verily, I – I alone – am God; there is no deity save Me. Hence, worship Me alone, and be constant in prayer, so as to remember Me!"

The Qur'an. Ta Ha (O Man) 20:14.

Quakers:

I saw that it was an easy matter to say death reigned from Adam to Moses; and that the law and the prophets were until John; and that the least in the kingdom is greater than John; but none could know how death reigned from Adam to Moses, etc. but by the same Holy Spirit that Moses and the prophets and John were in. Unless they had the Spirit and light of Jesus; how could they know the words of Christ without His Spirit?

George Fox, *The Journal of George Fox,* "Christ Fulfills all Types," 1649. P. 19.

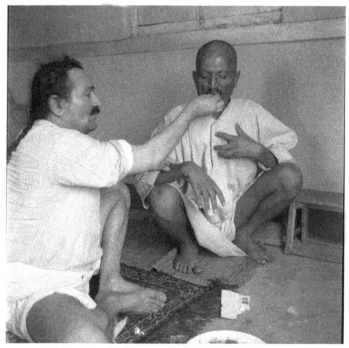

Meher Baba feeding Lakhan Shah in the Rahuri Cabin,
Lower Meherabad, India, early June 1939

SECTION FOUR

PROPER CONDUCT

Meher Baba, ca. 1934-1935, Upper Meherabad, India

PRINCIPLE 22

LONGING FOR TRUTH
AND UNION

22. Longing

If you experience that same longing and thirst for union with Me as one who has been lying for days in the hot sun of the Sahara experiences the longing for water, then you will realize Me.

Meher Baba:

> Open your heart by weeding out all desires and by harboring only one longing—the longing for union with the ultimate Reality.

> Meher Baba, *Discourses*, revised 6th edition, vol. I, pp. 19-20.

> As the fish which is taken out of the water longs to go back in the water, the aspirant who has perceived the goal longs to be united with God.

> Meher Baba, *Discourses*, revised 6th edition, vol. II, p. 9.

Zarathushtra:

As Thy true worshipper, in Knowledge firm,
    With all my heart, Thy Spirit Holiest
    For His protecting grace do I invoke;
I will fulfil the guardianship He planned;
    So, God, I would ask of Thee
    A vision of Thyself and speech with Thee.

The Divine Songs of Zarathushtra. Ahunavaiti 6.6—Yasna
33.6.

Krishna:

He who faithfully serves me
with the yoga of devotion, going
beyond the three gunas, is ready
to attain the ultimate freedom.

Bhagavad Gita. 14.26.

Tanakh:

How long, O Lord; will You ignore me forever?
How long will You hide Your face from me?
How long will I have cares on my mind,
    grief in my heart all day?
How long will my enemy have the upper hand?
Look at me, answer me, O Lord, my God!

Tanakh: The Holy Scriptures. Psalms 13:2–4.

Buddha:

> He in whom a desire for the Ineffable has sprung up,
> whose mind is permeated by this desire and whose
> thoughts are not bewildered by sensuality, is said to be
> 'bound up-stream.'

The Dhammapada. 16:218.

Jesus:

> But if any man love God, the same is known of him.

1 Corinthians 8:3 (AV).

> "And thou shalt love the Lord thy God with all thy heart,
> and with all thy soul, and with all thy mind, and with all thy
> strength: this is the first commandment."

Mark 12:30 (AV).

Muhammad's Revelation:

> O Mankind! Worship your Sustainer, who has created you
> and those who lived before you, so that you might remain
> conscious of Him who has made the earth a resting-place
> for you and the sky a canopy, and has sent down water
> from the sky and thereby brought forth fruits for your
> sustenance: do not, then, claim that there is any power
> that could rival God, when you know [that He is One].

The Qur'an. Al-Baqarah (The Cow) 2:21–22.

Quakers:

To forward this work the all-wise God is sometimes
pleased, through outward distress, to bring us near the
gates of death; that life being painful and afflicting, and
the prospect of eternity opened before us, all earthly
bonds may be loosened, and the mind prepared for that
deep and sacred instruction which otherwise would not
be received.

John Woolman, *The Journal of John Woolman* (HC), 1756. P.
198.

Meher Baba's beloved Mehera Irani, ca. 1938, Upper Meherabad, India

PRINCIPLE 23

PEACE OF MIND

23. Peace of mind

If you have the peace of a frozen lake, then too you will realize Me.

Meher Baba:

> Realisation of the unity of all is accompanied by peace and unfathomable bliss.
>
> Meher Baba, *Discourses*, revised 6th edition, vol. I, p. 19.
>
> Selfness for all brings about undisturbed harmony without loss of discrimination, and unshakable peace without indifference to the surroundings.
>
> Meher Baba, *Discourses*, revised 6th edition, vol. I, p. 19.

Zarathushtra:

> Thou art Divine, I know, O Lord Supreme,
> Since Good found entrance to my heart through Love,
> This taught me that for steady inner growth
> Quiet and silent meditation's best.
>
> *The Divine Songs of Zarathushtr*a. Ustavaiti 1.15—Yasna 43.15.

Krishna:

> Indifferent to scriptures, your mind
> stands by itself, unmoving,
> absorbed in deep meditation.
> This is the essence of yoga.

Bhagavad Gita. 2.53.

> The man whom desires enter
> as rivers flow into the sea,
> filled yet always unmoving—
> that man finds perfect peace.

Bhagavad Gita. 2.70.

Tanakh:

> For thus said my Lord God,
> The Holy One of Israel,
> "You shall triumph by stillness and quiet;
> Your victory shall come about
> Through calm and confidence."

Tanakh: The Holy Scriptures. Isaiah 30:15.

> I am ever mindful of the Lord's presence;
>   He is at my right hand; I shall never be shaken.
> So my heart rejoices,
>   my whole being exults,
>   and my body rests secure.

Tanakh: The Holy Scriptures. Psalms 16:8–9.

Buddha:

Wise people, after they have listened to the laws, become serene like a deep, clear and still lake.

The Dhammapada. 6:82.

Even though a speech be composed of a thousand words, but words without sense, one word of sense is better, which if a man hears he becomes quiet. Even though a stanza be composed of a thousand words but words without sense, one word of a stanza is better which if a man hears, he becomes quiet. Though a man recite a hundred stanzas made up of senseless words, one word of the Law is better, which if a man hears, he becomes quiet.

The Dhammapada. 8:100–102.

Jesus:

"Peace I leave with you, my peace I give unto you: not as the world giveth, give I unto you. Let not your heart be troubled, neither let it be afraid."

John 14:27 (AV).

Muhammad's Revelation:

O you who have attained to faith! Seek aid in steadfast patience and prayer: for, behold, God is with those who are patient in adversity…. And most certainly shall We try you by means of danger, and hunger, and loss of worldly goods, of lives and of [labour's] fruits. But give glad tidings unto those who are patient in adversity – who, when calamity befalls them, say, "Verily, unto God do we belong and, verily, unto Him we shall return."

The Qur'an. Al-Baqarah (The Cow) 2:153–156.

"Hence, we shall certainly bear with patience whatever hurt you may do us: for, all who have trust [in His existence] must place their trust in God [alone]!"

The Qur'an. Ibrahim (Abraham) 14:12.

Quakers:

Take heed of many words; what reaches to the life, settles in the life. That which comes from the life, and is received from God reaches to the life, and settles others in the life.

George Fox, *The Journal of George Fox*, "Sermon at John Crooks," 1658. P. 169.

De'la ta'ma ma'bor az lot'fe bi ne'ha'ya'te dust,
Cho la'fe eshgh za'di sar be'baz cha'bo'ko chost.

Oh Heart! Of the endless kindness of the Friend
hope, sever not,
When you boast of Love, quickly and
instantly you have bet your head.

Hafiz

PRINCIPLE 24

HUMILITY

24. Humility

If you have the humility of earth, which can be molded into any shape, then you will know Me.

Meher Baba:

> Even a small gift, given with humility and utterly unselfish love, is endowed with a much greater spiritual value.
>
> Meher Baba, *Discourses*, revised 6th edition, vol. I, p. 173.
>
> In the world of spirituality, humility counts at least as much as utility.
>
> Meher Baba, *Discourses*, revised 6th edition, vol. III, p. 133.

Zarathushtra:

> All Holy Lives are put into Thy Hands,
>   All that have been, and all that are today,
>   And all, O God, that shall ever be;
> Out of Thy Grace permit us these to share;
>   Through Love of Man, through Service and
> through Truth,

Raise Thou our Souls into Thy Realms of Light.

The Divine Songs of Zarathushtra. Ahunavaiti 6.10—Yasna 33.10.

Krishna:

> Humility, patience, sincerity,
> nonviolence, uprightness, purity,
> devotion to one's spiritual teacher,
> constancy, self-control ...
>
> all this is called true knowledge;
> what differs from it is called ignorance.

Bhagavad Gita. 13.7, 11.

> ... dignity, kindness, courage,
> a benevolent, loving heart—
> these are the qualities of men
> born with divine traits, Arjuna.

Bhagavad Gita. 16.3.

Tanakh:

> "Your hands shaped and fashioned me,
> Then destroyed every part of me.
> Consider that You fashioned me like clay;
> Will you then turn me back into dust?"

Tanakh: The Holy Scriptures. Job 10:8–9.

Buddha:

> Such a man who does his duty is tolerant like the earth, like a stone set in a threshold; he is like a lake without mud; no new births are in store for him.

The Dhammapada. 7:95.

> Irrigators guide the water (wherever they like); fletchers bend the arrow; carpenters bend a log of wood; good people fashion themselves.

The Dhammapada. 10:145.

Jesus:

> "And I say unto you, Make to yourselves friends of the mammon of unrighteousness; that, when ye fail, they may receive you into everlasting habitations. He that is faithful in that which is least is faithful also in much: and he that is unjust in the least is unjust also in much. If therefore ye have not been faithful in the unrighteous mammon, who will commit to your trust the true riches? And if ye have not been faithful in that which is another man's, who shall give you that which is your own? No servant can serve two masters: for either he will hate the one, and love the other; or else he will hold to the one, and despise the other. Ye cannot serve God and mammon."

Luke 16:9–13 (AV).

Humble yourselves therefore under the mighty hand of God, that he may exalt you in due time: Casting all your care upon him; for he careth for you.

1 Peter 5:6–7 (AV).

Muhammad's Revelation:

Behold, God does not disdain to propound a parable of a gnat, or of something [even] less than that. Now, as for those who have attained to faith, they know that it is the truth from their Sustainer – whereas those who are bent on denying the truth say, "What could [your] God mean by this parable?"

The Qur'an. Al-Baqarah (The Cow) 2:26.

Quakers:

Deep humility is a strong bulwark, and as we enter into it we find safety and true exaltation. The foolishness of God is wiser than man, and the weakness of God is stronger than man. Being unclothed of our own wisdom, and knowing the abasement of the creature, we find that power to arise that gives health and vigour to us.

John Woolman, *The Journal of John Woolman* (HC), 1756. P. 199.

حدیث هول قیامت که گفت واعظ شهر
کنایتیست که از روزگار هجران گفت

Ha'dise hou'le Quyamat ke goft, va'e'ze shahr
Ke'na'ya'tist ke az ruz'gar'e hej'ran goft

The tale of terror of the Resurrection Day, which the city
admonisher uttered,
Is just a small hint of the terror of separation from you ...
which he uttered.

Hafiz

PRINCIPLE 25

DESPERATION/PASSION

25. Desperation

If you experience the desperation that causes a person to commit suicide and you feel that you cannot live without seeing Me, then you will see Me.

Meher Baba:

> Divine desperateness is the beginning of spiritual awakening because it gives rise to the aspiration for God-realization.

> Meher Baba, *Discourses*, revised 6th edition, vol. II, p. 6.

> When the psychic energy of a man is thus centered upon discovering the goal of life, he uses the power of desperateness creatively.

> Meher Baba, *Discourses*, revised 6th edition, vol. II, p. 5.

Zarathushtra:

> This do I ask, God, tell me true:
> Reveal Thy purpose, God, for my Soul;
>   I seek Thy Teachings true through Love,
>   Through Knowledge's Wisdom seek the Goal of Life;

With all my Soul Thy orders I'll obey,
And thus attain Thee and Eternal Light.

The Divine Songs of Zarathushtra. Ustavaiti 2.8—Yasna 44.8.

Krishna:

Those who love and revere me
With unwavering faith, always
Centering their minds on me—
They are the most perfect in yoga.

Bhagavad Gita. 12.2.

Concentrate every thought
on me alone; with a mind
fully absorbed, one-pointed,
you will live within me, forever.

Bhagavad Gita. 12.8.

Tanakh:

My soul is consumed with longing
For Your rules at all times.

Tanakh: The Holy Scriptures. Psalms 119:20.

Buddha:

The Lord Buddha continued: — Subhuti, should there be any good pious disciple, man or woman, who in his zeal to practice charity is willing to sacrifice his life in the morning, or at noon-tide, or in the evening, on as many occasions as there are grains of sand in the river Ganges, even if these occasions recur for a hundred thousand myriad kalpas, would his blessing and merit be great? It would be great indeed, Lord Buddha.

A Buddhist Bible. P. 96.

Jesus:

"Blessed are they which do hunger and thirst after righteousness: for they shall be filled."

Matthew 5:6 (AV).

Muhammad's Revelation:

… all who share in faith strive hard [in God's cause] with their possessions and their lives: and it is they whom the most excellent things await [in the life to come], and it is they, they who shall attain to a happy state! … this is the triumph supreme!

The Qur'an. At-Tawbah (Repentance) 9:88–89.

Quakers:

In the year 1648, as I was sitting in a Friend's house in
Nottinghamshire (for by this time the power of God had
opened the hearts of some to receive the word of life and
reconciliation) I saw there was a great crack to go
throughout the earth, and a great smoke to go as the
crack went; and that after the crack there should be great
shaking: this was the earth in people's hearts, which was
to be shaken before the seed of God was raised out of
the earth. And it was so; for the Lord's power began to
shake them, and great meetings we began to have, and a
mighty power and work of God there was amongst
people, to the astonishment of both people and priests.

George Fox, *The Journal of George Fox*, "Outward and
Inward Law," 1648. P. 13.

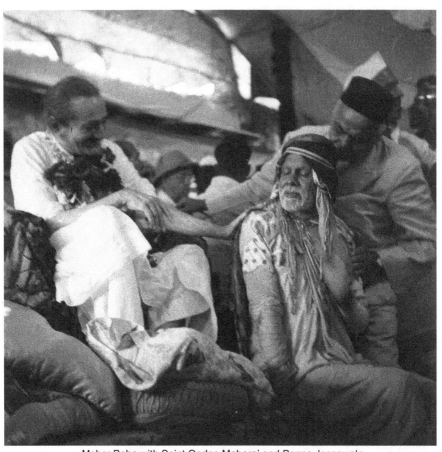

Meher Baba with Saint Gadge Maharaj and Pappa Jessawala,
September 12, 1954, Wadia Park, Ahmednagar, India

PRINCIPLE 26

FAITH

26. Faith

If you have the complete faith that Kalyan* had in his Master—in believing it was night although it was day because his Master said so—then you will know Me.

<u>Meher Baba:</u>

> The overflowing radiance of the Master's halo and the effulgence of his purity and compassion are mainly responsible for creating in the pupil an unswerving faith, which prepares him to follow the Master's orders implicitly—irrespective of their satisfying his critical spirit.

Meher Baba, *Discourses*, revised 6th edition, vol. I, p. 87.

> Complete self-surrender and unquestioning love become possible when the disciple achieves unswerving faith in the Master. Faith in the Master is an indispensable part of true discipleship.

Meher Baba, *Discourses*, revised 6th edition, vol. II, p. 39.

*Meher Baba then told another story about Swami Ramdas and Kalyan, which illustrated obedience: One day in broad daylight, Ramdas, saying it was dark out, told Kalyan to bring a lighted lantern, which he did immediately. Ramdas slapped him for this and said, "You fool! Can you not see it is daylight?" Kalyan apologized, asking for his forgiveness as he left with the lantern. By using this example, Ramdas explained to Shivaji about faith and obedience. Hafiz has said, "Whatever my Master says, I accept wholeheartedly without the slightest thought." This is implicit faith and abject obedience. But it is very, very difficult — rather impossible — particularly for you Westerners who have so much intellect — always arguing the merits and demerits of things. In Kalyan's case, he not only obeyed his Master's orders, but he actually believed Ramdas when he told him it was the darkness of night — even in broad daylight! Such belief and faith is truly impossible. *Lord Meher,* online rev. edition. P.

<u>Zarathushtra:</u>

I'll speak about the Greatest One of All,
Praising Him, Lord of Wisdom through His Truth,
And all the Lords of Wisdom that are His;
    May He through His Good Spirit hear our call,
    Through Love my Faith to Him I pledge,
    He in His Wisdom guides me to His Light.

The Divine Songs of Zarathushtra. Ustavaiti 3.6—Yasna 45.6.

<u>Krishna:</u>

Concentrate your mind on me,
fill your heart with my presence,
love me, serve me, worship me,
and you will attain me at last.

Bhagavad Gita. 9.34.

Those who love and revere me
with unwavering faith, always
centering their minds on me—
they are the most perfect in yoga.

Bhagavad Gita. 12.2.

Tanakh:

But now thus said the Lord—
Who created you, O Jacob,
Who formed you, O Israel:
Fear not, for I will redeem you;
I have singled you out by name,
You are Mine.
When you pass through water,
I will be with you;
Through streams,
They shall not overwhelm you.
When you walk through fire,
You shall not be scorched;
Through flame,
It shall not burn you.
For I the Lord am your God,
The Holy One of Israel, your Savior.

Tanakh: The Holy Scriptures. Isaiah 43:1–3.

Buddha:

Whoso pays homage to those who deserve homage,
whether the Awakened or their disciples, those who have
overcome the hosts of evils and crossed the flood of
sorrow, who have found deliverance and know no fear —
his merit can never be measured by anyone.

The Dhammapada. 14:195, 196.

The disciples of Gotama are always wide awake and watchful, and their thoughts day and night are ever set on Buddha.

The Dhammapada. 21:296.

Jesus:

And he spake a parable unto them to this end, that men ought always to pray, and not to faint.

Luke 18:1 (AV).

Muhammad's Revelation:

And say [in thy prayer]: "O my Sustainer! Cause me to enter [upon whatever I may do] in a manner true and sincere, and cause me to leave [it] in a manner true and sincere, and grant me, out of Thy grace, sustaining strength!"

The Qur'an. Al-Isrãa (The Night Journey) 17:80.

Verily, those who have attained to faith [in this divine writ], as well as those who follow the Jewish faith, and the Christians, and the Sabians – all whom believe in God and the Last Day and do righteous deeds – shall have their reward with their Sustainer; and no fear need they have, and neither shall they grieve.

The Qur'an. Al-Baqarah (The Cow) 2:62.

Quakers:

I awoke; it was yet dark, and no appearance of day or
moonshine, and as I opened my eyes I saw a Light in my
chamber, at the apparent distance of five feet, about nine
inches in diameter, of a clear easy brightness, and near its
center the most radiant. As I lay still looking upon it
without any surprise, words were spoken to my inward
ear, which filled my whole inward man. They were not the
effect of thought, nor any conclusion in relation to
appearance, but as the language of the Holy One spoken
in my mind. The words were CERTAIN EVIDENCE
OF DIVINE TRUTH. They were again repeated exactly
in the same manner, and then the Light disappeared.

John Woolman, *The Journal of John Woolman* (HC), 1758. P.
200.

منن زرجون و چه راد که بنده مقبل   قبول که در جان هر سخن که سلطان گفت

BEFITTING A FORTUNATE SLAVE CARRY OUT EVERY COMMAND OF THE MASTER, WITHOUT ANY QUESTION OF WHY AND WHAT.

پو بشنوی سخن اهل دل مگو که خطا ست   سخن شناس نئی جان دلبہ اینجا ست

ABOUT WHAT YOU HEAR FROM THE MASTER NEVER SAY IT IS WRONG BECAUSE MY DEAR, THE FAULT LIES IN YOUR OWN INCAPACITY TO UNDERSTAND HIM.

بنده پیر مغانم که ز جہلم بر ہاند   پیر ما هر چه کند عین رعایت باشد

I AM SLAVE OF THE MASTER, WHO HAS RELEASED ME FROM IGNORANCE, WHATEVER MY MASTER DOES IS OF THE HIGHEST BENEFIT TO ALL CONCERNED. حافظ—HAFIZ.

Three of Meher Baba's favorite couplets by Hafiz, translated from Persian by Baba Himself. They are framed and displayed in Mandali Hall, Meherazad, Meher Baba's home in India.

PRINCIPLE 27

FIDELITY

27. Fidelity

If you have the fidelity that your breath has in keeping you company till the end of your life—even without your constantly feeling it, both in happiness and suffering, never turning against you—then you will know Me.

Meher Baba:

> To avoid defeat, the mind must stick tenaciously to the right value which it has seen. Thus the solution of mental conflict requires not only perception of right values but also an unswerving fidelity to them.
>
> Meher Baba, *Discourses*, revised 6th edition, vol. II, pp. 61-62.

Zarathushtra:

> His favour will I seek and Love's,
> For in His Plan are found both weal and woe.
>
> *The Divine Songs of Zarathushtra*. Ustavaiti 3.9—Yasna 45.9.

Krishna:

Only by single-minded
devotion can I be known
as I truly am, Arjuna—
can I be seen and entered.

Bhagavad Gita. 11.54.

Those who love and revere me
with unwavering faith, always
centering their minds on me—
they are the most perfect in yoga.

Bhagavad Gita. 12.2.

Tanakh:

But ask the beasts, and they will teach you;
The birds of the sky, they will tell you,
Or speak to the earth, it will teach you;
The fish of the sea, they will inform you.
Who among all these does not know
That the hand of the Lord has done this?
In His hand is every living soul
And the breath of all mankind.

Tanakh: The Holy Scriptures. Job 12:7–10.

Buddha:

The disciples of Gotama are always wide awake and
watchful, and their thoughts day and night are ever set on
Buddha.
   The disciples of Gotama are always wide awake and
watchful, and their thoughts day and night are ever set on
the Law.
   The disciples of Gotama are always wide awake and
watchful, and their thoughts day and night are ever set on
the Order.
   The disciples of Gotama are always wide awake and
watchful, and their thoughts day and night are ever set on
the body.
   The disciples of Gotama are always wide awake and
watchful, and their mind day and night ever delights in
compassion.

The Dhammapada. 21:296–300.

Jesus:

"For verily I say unto you, Till heaven and earth pass, one
jot or one tittle shall in no wise pass from the law, till all
be fulfilled."

Matthew 5:18 (AV).

Muhammad's Revelation:

Verily, those who have attained to faith and do good
works, and are constant in prayer, and dispense charity –
they shall have their reward with their Sustainer, and no
fear need they have, and neither shall they grieve.

The Qur'an. Al-Baqarah (The Cow) 2:277.

And when Jesus became aware of their refusal to
acknowledge the truth, he asked: "Who will be my helpers
in God's cause?" The white-garbed ones replied: "We
shall be [thy] helpers [in the cause] of God! We believe in
God: and bear thou witness that we have surrendered
ourselves unto Him! O our Sustainer! We believe in what
Thou hast bestowed from on high, and we follow this
Apostle; make us one, then, with all who bear witness [to
the truth]!"

The Qur'an. Āl-Imrān (The House of ʿImrān) 3:52–53.

Quakers:

When we look towards the end of our life, and think on
the division of our substance among our successors, if
we know that it was collected in the fear of the Lord, in
honesty, inequity, and in uprightness of heart before Him,
we may consider it as His gift to us, and with a single eye
to his blessing, bestow it on those we leave behind us.
Such is the happiness of the plain ways of true virtue.
"The work of righteousness shall be peace; and the effect
of righteousness, quietness and assurance
forever." (Isaiah 22:17)

John Woolman, *The Journal of John Woolman* (HC), 1758. P.
211.

Dur ast sa're ab az in bad'di'ye, hosh dar,
Ta ghole bi'a'ban na'fari'bad be sa'ra'bat.

In this desert, the water pool is far. Keep sense!
So that the creatures of the desert, may not,
with the mirage, deceive thee.

Hafiz

PRINCIPLE 28

INTEREST IN SENSUAL INDULGENCE NATURALLY FALLS AWAY

28. Control through love

When your love for Me drives away your lust for the things of the senses, then you will realize Me.

<u>Meher Baba:</u>

> Though control might be difficult at the beginning, through sincere effort it gradually becomes natural and easy of achievement.
>
> Meher Baba, *Discourses*, revised 6th edition, vol. I, p. 72.
>
> Control which has true spiritual value does not consist in the mechanical repression of thoughts and desires, but is the natural restraint exercised by perception of positive values discovered during the process of experience.
>
> Meher Baba, *Discourses*, revised 6th edition, vol. I, p. 73.

Zarathushtra:

> The false prevents the Righteous everywhere
> From helping man along the upward Path;
> He worketh not as friend, is dangerous;
> Invite him not as helper in your work;
>> They who oppose him, God, heart and soul,
>> They are true Leaders, they obey Thy Will.

The Divine Songs of Zarathushtra. Ustavaiti 4.4—Yasna 46.4.

Krishna:

> When a man gives up all desires
> that emerge from the mind, and rests
> contented in the Self by the Self,
> he is called a man of firm wisdom.

Bhagavad Gita. 2.55.

> Restraining the senses, disciplined,
> he should focus his whole mind on me;
> when the senses are in his control,
> that man is a man of firm wisdom.

Bhagavad Gita. 2.61.

Tanakh:

"Come, let us reach an understanding,
—says the Lord.
Be your sins like crimson,
They can turn snow-white;
Be they red as dyed wool,
They can become like fleece."
If, then, you agree and give heed,
You will eat the good things of the earth."

Tanakh: The Holy Scriptures. Isaiah 1:18–19.

Buddha:

He who lives without looking for pleasures, his senses
well controlled, moderate in his food, faithful and strong,
him Māra will certainly not overthrow, any more than the
wind throws down a rock mountain.

The Dhammapada. 1.8.

If a man's thoughts are free from lust, if his mind is not
perplexed, if he has renounced merit and demerit, then
there is no fear from him while he is watchful.

The Dhammapada. 3.39.

Jesus:

> Blessed is the man that endureth temptation: for when
> he is tried, he shall receive the crown of life, which the
> Lord hath promised to them that love him. Let no man
> say when he is tempted, I am tempted of God: for God
> cannot be tempted with evil, neither tempteth he any
> man: But every man is tempted, when he is drawn away
> of his own lust, and enticed.

James 1:12–14 (AV).

> For to be carnally minded is death; but to be spiritually
> minded is life and peace.

Romans 8:6 (AV).

Muhammad's Revelation:

> Alluring unto man is the enjoyment of worldly desires
> through women, and children, and heaped-up treasures of
> gold and silver, and horses of high mark, and cattle, and
> lands. All this may be enjoyed in the life of this world –
> But the most beauteous of all goals is with God....For
> the God-conscious there are, with their Sustainer, gardens
> through which running waters flow, therein to abide, and
> spouses pure, and God's goodly acceptance.

The Qur'an. Ãl-Imran (The House of Imran) 3:14–15.

Quakers:

> I heard that the case for slavery was coming to Yearly Meeting. This brought a weighty exercise upon me, and under a sense of my own infirmities, and the great danger of turning aside from perfect purity, my mind was often drawn to retire alone, and put up my prayers to the Lord that he would be graciously pleased to strengthen me; that setting aside all views of self interest and the friendship of this world, I might stand fully resigned to His holy will.

John Woolman, *The Journal Of John Woolman* (HC), 1758. P. 224.

"Eternal Wealth"

بُرو کار میکُن مگو چیست کار برو کار میکُن

که سرمایهٔ جاودانی است کار

Buro kar mekon magu chist kar,

Ke sarmaye javedani ast kar.

Go and do some work, do not question why to work

Since to work is to earn the eternal asset and real wealth

سعدی   Saadi

Translation by Mehernoush McPherson

PRINCIPLE 29

SELFLESS SERVICE

29. Selfless Service

If you have the quality of selfless service unaffected by results similar to that of the sun, which serves the world by shining on all creation—on the grass in the field, on the birds in the air, on the beasts in the forest, on all of mankind with its sinners and saints, its rich and poor—unmindful of the attitude toward it, then you will win Me.

<u>Meher Baba:</u>

> Selfless service is accomplished when there is not the slightest thought of reward or result, and when there is complete disregard of one's own comfort or convenience or the possibility of being misunderstood.

Meher Baba, *Discourses*, revised 6th edition, vol. I, p. 79.

> The real justification for a life of selfless service is to be found in this intrinsic worth of such a life and not in any ulterior result or consequence.

Meher Baba, *Discourses*, revised 6th edition, vol. II, p. 207.

Zarathushtra:

> The strong wise man, guided by Law Divine,
> Or by his human heart, kindly receives
> All suppliants who come, though they be False.

> *The Divine Songs of Zarathushtra.* Ustavaiti 4.5—Yasna 46.5.

Krishna:

> With no desire for success,
> no anxiety about failure,
> indifferent to results, he burns up
> his actions in the fire of wisdom.

> *Bhagavad Gita.* 4.19.

> He who performs his duty
> with no concern for results
> is the true man of yoga—not
> he who refrains from action.

> *Bhagavad Gita.* 6.1.

Tanakh:

> The path of the righteous is like radiant sunlight,
> Ever brightening until noon.

> *Tanakh: The Holy Scriptures.* Proverbs 4:18

No longer shall you need the sun
For light by day,
Nor the shining of the moon
For radiance [by night];
For the Lord shall be your light everlasting,
Your God shall be your glory.
Your sun shall set no more,
Your moon no more withdraw;
For the Lord shall be a light to you forever.

Tanakh: The Holy Scriptures. Isaiah 60:19–20

Buddha:

He whose misdeeds are covered by good deeds, brightens up this world, like the moon when freed from clouds.

The Dhammapada. 13:173.

The disciples of Gotama are always wide awake and watchful, and their mind day and night ever delights in compassion.

The Dhammapada. 21:300.

Jesus:

My little children, let us not love in word, neither in tongue; but in deed and in truth. And hereby we know that we are of the truth, and shall assure our hearts before him.

1 John 3:18–19 (AV).

Muhammad's Revelation:

The parable of those who spend their possessions for the sake of God is that of a grain out of which grows seven ears, in every ear a hundred grains: for God grants manifold increase unto whom He wills; and God is infinite, all-knowing. They who spend their possessions for the sake of God and do not thereafter mar their spending by stressing their own benevolence and hurting [the feelings of the needy] shall have their reward with their Sustainer, and no fear need they have, and neither shall they grieve. A kind word and the veiling of another's want is better than a charitable deed followed by hurt.

The Qur'an. Al-Baqarah (The Cow) 2:261–263.

Quakers:

This meeting lasted three days, and many friends from most parts of the nation came to it; so that the inns and towns around were filled, for many thousands of people came over all, and a glorious meeting it was. The everlasting gospel was preached, and many received it, which brought life and immortality to light in them, and shined over all.

George Fox, *The Journal of George Fox*, "Sermon at John Crooks," 1658. P. 169.

Meher Baba, Toka, India, 1928

PRINCIPLE 30

RENUNCIATION

30. Renunciation

If you renounce for Me everything physical, mental, and spiritual, then you will have Me.

Meher Baba:

> Renunciation of desires does not mean asceticism or a merely negative attitude to life....It is a positive attitude of releasing all that is good, noble, and beautiful in man. It also contributes to all that is gracious and lovely in the environment.

> Meher Baba, *Discourses*, revised 6th edition, vol. I, p. 20.

> Only by treading the path of inner and spontaneous renunciation of craving is it possible to attain true freedom and unity.

> Meher Baba, *Discourses*, revised 6th edition, vol. I, p. 148.

Zarathushtra:

> She is indeed our Refuge safe; She brings
> Soul-Strength and Life-renewed, twin gifts of Love;
>   God hath covered Her with food for man,

She feedeth all mankind since dawn of Life;
Such is God's Plan—and Knowledge's Law.

The Divine Songs of Zarathushtra. Spenta-Mainyu 2.6—
Yasna 48.6.

Krishna:

Calmly renouncing all actions,
the embodied Self dwells at ease
as lord of the nine-gated city,
not acting, not causing action.

Bhagavad Gita. 5.13.

Self-mastered, with mind unattached
at all times, beyond desire,
one attains through renunciation
the supreme freedom from action.

Bhagavad Gita. 18.49.

Tanakh:

Into Your hand I entrust my spirit;
    You redeem me, O Lord, faithful God.

Tanakh: The Holy Scriptures. Psalms 31:6.

Show favor to Your servant;
    As You are faithful, deliver me.

Tanakh: The Holy Scriptures. Psalms 31:17.

Buddha:

Those whose minds are well-grounded in the (seven) elements of knowledge, who rejoice in the renunciation of affections and in freedom from attachments, whose evil proclivities have been overcome and who are full of light, are completely liberated even in this world.

The Dhammapada. 6:89.

There is no suffering for him who has finished his journey, and abandoned grief, who has freed himself on all sides, and thrown off all fetters.

The Dhammapada. 7:90.

Jesus:

"Lay not up for yourselves treasures upon earth, where moth and rust doth corrupt, and where thieves break through and steal: But lay up for yourselves treasures in heaven, where neither moth nor rust doth corrupt, and where thieves do not break through nor steal: For where your treasure is, there will your heart be also."

Matthew 6:19–21 (AV).

Muhammad's Revelation:

Yea, indeed: everyone who surrenders his whole being unto God, and is a doer of good withal, shall have his reward with his Sustainer; and all such need have no fear, and neither shall they grieve.

The Qur'an. Al-Baqarah (The Cow) 2:112.

Quakers:

I then heard a soft melodious voice, more pure and
harmonious that any I had heard with my ears before; I
believed it was an angel who spoke to other angels the
words "John Wollman is dead." Then the mystery was
opened and I perceived there was joy in heaven over a
sinner who had repented, and that the language "John
Woolman is dead" meant no more than the death of my
own will.

John Woolman, *The Journal of John Woolman* (HC), 1772. P.
306.

Jahan ni'yan hame gar man'e man ko'nand as eshgh,
Goftam kho'sha hava'yi, kaz ba'de sobh khi'zad.

If all the people of the world forbid me Love,
That which the Lord commands, I shall do.

Hafiz

PRINCIPLE 31

OBEDIENCE TO WHAT YOU KNOW TO BE TRUE

31. Obedience

If your obedience is as spontaneous, complete, and natural as light is to the eye or smell is to the nose, then you will come to Me.

Meher Baba:

> Literal obedience is the effect of the rocklike faith and deep love which the Master inspires in the pupil through his human appeal.

Meher Baba, *Discourses*, revised 6th edition, vol. I, p. 87.

> Through such implicit and unquestioning obedience, all the crooked knots of your desires and sanskaras are set straight. It is also through such obedience that a deep link is created between the Master and the pupil, with the result that there is an unhindered and perennial flow of spiritual wisdom and power into the pupil.

Meher Baba, *Discourses*, revised 6th edition, vol. I, p. 87.

Zarathushtra:

Such are, indeed, the Saviours of the Earth,
They follow Duty's call, the call of Love :
God, they listen unto Love;
   They do what Knowledge bids, and Thy Commands;
   Surely they are the Vanquishers of Hate.

The Divine Songs of Zarathushtra. Spenta-Mainyu 2.12—
Yasna 48.12.

Krishna:

Those who realize the essence
of duty, who trust me completely
and surrender their lives to me—
I love them with very great love.

Bhagavad Gita. 12.20.

Tanakh:

"Does the Lord delight in burnt offerings and sacrifices
As much as in obedience to the Lord's command?
Surely, obedience is better than sacrifice,
Compliance than the fat of rams."

Tanakh: The Holy Scriptures. 1 Samuel 15:22.

But let all who seek You be glad and rejoice in You;
let those who are eager for Your deliverance always say,
"Extolled be God!"

Tanakh: The Holy Scriptures. Psalms 70:5.

Buddha:

> Rouse thyself by thyself, examine thyself by thyself; thus self-guarded and mindful, wilt thou, O monk, live happily. For self is the lord of self, self is the refuge of self, therefore curb thyself as the merchant curbs a good horse.

The Dhammapada. 25:379–380.

Jesus:

> "Therefore whosoever heareth these sayings of mine, and doeth them, I will liken him unto a wise man, which built his house upon a rock: And the rain descended, and the floods came, and the winds blew, and beat upon that house; and it fell not: for it was founded upon a rock."

Matthew 7:24–25 (AV).

Muhammad's Revelation:

> And God's [alone] are the attributes of perfection; invoke Him, then, by these, and stand aloof from all who distort the meaning of His attributes: they shall be requited for all that they were wont to do! Now, among those whom We have created there are people who guide [others] in the way of the truth and act justly in its light. But as for those who are bent on giving the lie to Our messages – We shall bring them low, step by step, without their perceiving how it came about: for, behold, though I may give them rein for a while, My subtle scheme is exceedingly firm!

The Qur'an. Al- Arif (The Faculty of Discernment) 7:180–183.

Quakers:

In this case I had fresh confirmation that acting contrary to present outward interest, from a motive of Divine love, and in regard to truth and righteousness, and thereby incurring the resentments of people, opens the way to a treasure better than silver, and to a friendship exceeding the friendship of men.

John Woolman, *The Journal of John Woolman* (HC), 1753. P. 189.

یار نماند آنکه با یار ب ساخت   مفلس نشد انکی با خریدار ب
ساخت بی
مه نور اذان گرفت ، کز شب نر میده   کل بری اذان یافت که با خان ب
ساخت

The one who conforms to the Friend
will never be left friendless,
And the one who conforms to the customer
will never be bankrupt.
The moon obtains light when not frightened
away by the darkness of the night,
The rose acquires fragrance when it gets used to the thorn.

Jalal al-Din Rumi

PRINCIPLE 32

SURRENDER
WHOLEHEARTEDLY
AND WITHOUT FEAR

32. Surrenderance

If your surrenderance to Me is as wholehearted as that of one who, suffering from insomnia, surrenders to sudden sleep without fear of being lost, then you will have Me.

Meher Baba:

> Complete self-surrender and unquestioning love become possible when the disciple achieves unswerving faith in the Master.

> Meher Baba, *Discourses*, revised 6th edition, vol. II, p. 39.

> Spiritual advancement is a succession of one surrender after another until the goal of the final surrenderance of the separate ego-life is completely achieved.... Therefore, in a sense, the most complete surrenderance to the Master is equivalent to the attainment of the Truth, which is the ultimate goal of all spiritual advancement.

> Meher Baba, *Discourses*, revised 6th edition, vol. II, p. 198.

Zarathushtra:

> But, God, he who through the urge of heart,
> Through sacrifice of Self, doth link himself,
> And his own Inner Self with Love,
>> Finds Wisdom, and Knowledge's Wisdom, too;
>> Sheltered by Righteousness, he shall dwell with Them.

The Divine Songs of Zarathushtra. Spenta-Mainyu 3.5—
Yasna 49.5.

Krishna:

> Surrendering all thoughts of outcome,
> unperturbed, self-reliant,
> he does nothing at all, even
> when fully engaged in actions.

Bhagavad Gita. 4.20.

> Those who realize the essence
> of duty, who trust me completely
> and surrender their lives to me—
> I love them with very great love.

Bhagavad Gita. 12.20.

Tanakh:

> Now do not be stiff necked like your fathers; submit yourselves to the Lord and come to His sanctuary, which He consecrated forever, and serve the Lord your God ... for the Lord your God is gracious and merciful; He will not turn His face from you if you return to Him.
>
> *Tanakh: The Holy Scripture.* 2 Chronicles 30:8–9.

Buddha:

> His thought is quiet, quiet are his words and deed, when he has obtained freedom by true knowledge, when he has thus become a quiet man.
>
> *The Dhammapada.* 7:96.

Jesus:

> If any man will come after me, let him deny himself and take up his cross and follow me. For whosoever will save his life shall lose it: and whosoever will lose his life for my sake will find it.
>
> Matthew 16:24-26 (KJV).

Muhammad's Revelation:

Yea, indeed: everyone who surrenders his whole being
unto God, and is a doer of good withal, shall have his
reward with his Sustainer; and all such need have no fear,
and neither shall they grieve.

The Qur'an. Al-Baqarah (The Cow) 2:112.

Behold the only [true] religion in the sight of God is
[man's] self-surrender unto Him ... Thus, [O Prophet,] if
they argue with thee, say, "I have surrendered my whole
being unto God, and [so have] all who follow me!" – and
ask those who have been vouchsafed revelation aforetime,
as well as all unlettered people, "Have you [too]
surrendered yourself unto Him?" And if they surrender
themselves unto Him, they are on the right path.

The Qur'an. Al-Imran (The House of Imran) 3:19–20.

Quakers:

I remembered that thou art omnipotent, that I had called
thee Father, and I felt that I loved thee, and was made
quiet in thy will, and I waited for deliverance from thee;
thou hadst pity upon me when no man could help me; I
saw that meekness under suffering was shown to us in the
most affecting example of thy Son, and thou taught me
to follow him, and I said, "Thy will, O Father be done."

John Woolman's last words, 1772, *The Journal of John
Woolman* (HC). P. 314.

Meher Baba with Mehera, Khorshed, and Naja, Upper Meherabad, 1936

PRINCIPLE 33

LOVING WITHOUT WANTING ANYTHING IN RETURN

33. Love

If you have that love for Me that Saint Francis had for Jesus, then not only will you realize Me but you will please Me.

<u>Meher Baba:</u>

> Love is therefore rightly regarded as being the most important avenue leading to the realisation of the Highest. In love the soul is completely absorbed in the Beloved and is therefore detached from the actions of the body or mind.

Meher Baba, *Discourses*, revised 6th edition, vol. I, p. 80.

> Through the intensity of this ever growing love, he eventually breaks through the shackles of the self and becomes united with the Beloved. This is the consummation of love. When love has thus found its fruition, it has become divine.

Meher Baba, *Discourses*, revised 6th edition, vol. I, p. 167.

> There is no sadhana [practice, striving, endeavor; directing toward the goal] greater than love, there is no law higher than love, and there is no goal that is beyond love—for

love in its divine state becomes infinite. God and love are identical, and one who has divine love already has God.

Meher Baba, *Discourses*, revised 6th edition, vol. II, p. 208

Zarathushtra:

> With chants that well up from my Inmost Heart,
> With hands uplifted, God, I beseech,
>> That I, Thy humble Lover, Thee attain,
>> Come closer unto Thee through Knowledge's help,
>> Through Love's wonder-working Love.

The Divine Songs of Zarathushtra. Spenta-Mainyu 4.8—
Yasna 50.8.

Krishna:

> Even the heartless criminal,
> if he loves me with all his heart,
> will certainly grow into sainthood
> as he moves toward me on this path.

Bhagavad Gita. 9.30.

> All those who love and trust me,
> even the lowest of the low—
> prostitutes, beggars, slaves—
> will attain the ultimate goal.

Bhagavad Gita. 9.32.

Tanakh:

> Then the Lord your God will open up your heart and the
> hearts of your offspring to love the Lord your God with
> all your heart and soul, in order that you may live... For
> the Lord will again delight in your well being.

Tanakh: The Holy Scriptures. Deuteronomy 30:6, 9.

> Those who love me I love,
> And those who seek me will find me ...
> My fruit is better than gold, fine gold,
> And my produce better than choice silver ...
> I endow those who love me with substance.

Tanakh: The Holy Scriptures. Proverbs 8:17, 19, 21.

Buddha:

> The true Samana, he who is seeking the way to the
> Brahma World, lets his mind pervade all quarters of the
> world with thoughts of Love; first one quarter then the
> second quarter, then the third quarter and so the fourth
> quarter. And thus the whole wide world, above, below,
> around, and everywhere, does he continue to pervade
> with thoughts of love, far-reaching, beyond measure, all-
> embracing.

A Buddhist Bible. P. 71.

<u>Jesus:</u>

"And thou shalt love the Lord thy God with all thy heart, and with all thy soul, and with all thy mind, and with all thy strength: this is the first commandment. And the second is like, namely, Thou shalt love thy neighbour as thyself. There is none other commandment greater than these."

Mark 12:30–31 (AV).

Beloved, let us love one another: for love is of God; and every one that loveth is born of God, and knoweth God. He that loveth not knoweth not God; for God is love.

1 John 4:7–8 (AV).

<u>Muhammad's Revelation:</u>

And [thus it was that Jesus always said], "Verily, God is my Sustainer as well as your Sustainer; so worship [none but] Him: this [alone] is a straight way."

The Qur'an. Marayam (Mary) 19:36.

But those who shall have attained to faith and done righteous deeds will be brought into gardens through which running waters flow, therein to abide by their Sustainer's leave, and will be welcomed with the greeting, "Peace!"

The Qur'an. Ibrâhim (Abraham) 14:23.

33. LOVING WITHOUT WANTING ANYTHING

Quakers:

Would God this Divine Virtue were more implanted and diffused among mankind, the pretenders to Christianity especially, and we should certainly mind piety more than controversy, and exercise Love and Compassion instead of censuring and persecuting one another in any manner whatsoever.

William Penn, *More Fruits of Solitude*, "Of Charity," 1682. (Boston, Massachusetts: Harvard Press, 1927), p. 395.

ACKNOWLEDGMENTS

First and foremost, thank you to Meher Baba, the Awakener, the One who comes again and again, again and again, again, and again, and still yet again. He awakens us to His mercy, understanding, and righteousness (the Three Yogas) faithfully and consistently age after age.

Thanks to Laurent Weichberger, who chided me as we sat in Sheriar Books: "We do not want to be the guys ten years from now who say ... 'We really should have done this work.'"

To Sheila Gambill, for her insistence on editing accuracy and absolute faithfulness to Meher Baba's original language, a hearty thank you. I asked Hafiz how her contribution could possibly be captured in words, and he replied:

"Recast a world with new design,
With carefree souls, with love divine.
And if the warring hosts of grief and woe
Invade again to slay the lover's heart, I know 'tis time,
O Saki belle of mine,
'Tis time we blend our wits, our strengths combine,
Misfortune's soldiers bluntly meet and end them in defeat."
   The Ghazaliyyat of Haafez of Shiraz,
   Mehdi Nakosteen trans., number 87.

And furthermore, in praise of Sheilaji's work ethic:
"In the world, not I alone am distressed from
   being without work,
For learning without doing, is the grief is the learned."
   The Divan-I-Hafiz,
   H. Wilberforce Clarke trans., number 47.

In praise of Sheilaji's convincement of Interfaith work, Hafiz said:

"The way of graciousness and of kindness,
Altogether is the gift of the true Beloved:
Whether the Muslim rosary He ordered; or,
   the Christian cord, He brought."
The Complete Ghazals of Hafez Volume 2,
Sajjad Khojasteh trans., number 146.

To Patty Robinson, clerk of the Quaker Clearness Committee, who found Unity with this work as led by The Holy Spirit. We are grateful for her clerking and for taking the time to meet with Susan and me before the Clearness process began.

Gratitude to Peter Meredith, who presented this leading to Annapolis Monthly Friends Business Meeting for Unity. Also, thank thee Friend, for alternating clerking the Worship services once the pandemic arrived, when Annapolis Friends went to digital Worship.

To the Community of Friends at Annapolis Friends Monthly Meeting, for the unexpected ease in finding Unity on this work as led by the Spirit. There was no "herding of cats," which is so often one of the delights of our Religious Society. My heart feels such support from the consensus of confidence that now holds this tenderly as an "Embraced Quaker Ministry."

To "Freedom" Francis Wayne, also a member of the Quaker Clearness Committee, as he prepares to go as a lay minister to South Sudan with Mary Knoll Lay Ministers, a heartfelt Jai Baba!!!

To Reverend Chris Holmes of the United Methodist Church, who refused to take his fees for coaching because "this is God's work," Amen and Alleluia! Also, we agree that Justice is not "Just Us."

To Patrick Nugent, a Recorded Minister within Friends United Meeting, for his Unity with this work from a Christian Minister's perspective.

Praise To Nicole Smile, also a member of the Quaker Clearness Committee, for her never-ceasing encouragement and for taking the detailed minutes, in good Quaker Order, for all our Saturday meetings.

Praise to Susan Wolfe, for her dear, dear Love for Baba and for me, and for her patience when this work made demands on our personal time together.

To Mehernoush McPherson, my *Amouzagar* (Teacher) of Farsi, thanks for finding and translating Hafiz ... ever wine-soaked in Unity with all who Love.

To Cliff Hackford, the Briarcliff Guy, for the incredible Middle Eastern version of the three Zoroastrian prayers.

To Azita Namiranian, thanks for ensuring the accuracy of the quotes from *The Divine Songs of Zarathustra*.

Words fail me in praise of Karl Moeller for his attention to detail in working together for the Unity of the Good News. This *Bayt* (two-line verse), a gift from the Immortal Hafiz, is in praise of Karl's work. These lines, that as Shelley says, "leave the whole untold," also speak my heart to the disputation over quoting the seventh edition versus the sixth revised edition of Meher Baba's *Discourses*. These lines were translated by Mehernoush McPherson.

طاق و رواق مدرسه و قال و قیل علم
The arch and columns in school and
disputation and cacophony of learning
در راه جام و ساقی مه رو نهاده ایم
We have placed in the path of pure wine
and the Beloved wine giver with face soft as the moon

Finally, Praise and Glory to

Asho Zarathushtra
Shri Krishna,
Lord Buddha,
the Jewish Prophets of the Tanakh,
Jesus Christ,
Rasulallah Muhammad,
for their words recorded in Unity with
Avatar Meher Baba.

PHOTO CREDITS

Cover   Meher Baba in Ahmednagar or Meherabad, circa 1925. Photographer: G.M. Shah. Courtesy of Meher Nazar Publications.

Page iv   Original painting by Vanessa Weichberger, "Meher Baba, the White Horse Avatar." Courtesy and ©Vanessa Weichberger.

4   Meher Baba in the doorway of the Rahuri Cabin, Lower Meherabad, India, circa 1938. Photographer unknown. Courtesy of Meher Nazar Publications.

17   Al-Nur Mosque, Christchurch, New Zealand.

22   Meher Baba, Meherabad, India, circa 1926-27. Photographer unknown. Mehera once remarked that this was her favorite photo of Baba. Courtesy of Meher Nazar Publications.

34   Michaelangelo's Pieta, Rome.

40   Upasni Maharaj, Sakori, India. Photographer unknown. Courtesy of Meher Nazar Publications.

58   Francis Brabazon, Guruprasad, Pune, India. Photographer: Meelan. Courtesy of Meher Nazar Publications.

64   Meher Baba signing front pages of *God Speaks*, Satara, India, March 18, 1955. Photographer: Mani. Courtesy of Meher Nazar Publications.

66   Meher Baba at Guruprasad, Pune, India, November 1962. Photographer: Meelan. Courtesy of Meher Nazar Publications.

72   Cage Room, Upper Meherabad, India, July 30, 1941.
      Photographer: Padri. Courtesy of Meher Nazar
      Publications.

78   Saint Francis fresco detail.

84   Meher Baba with Shariat Khan, a third-plane *mast*,
      Bangalore, India, January 1940. Photographer: Padri.
      Courtesy of Meher Nazar Publications.

90   Meher Baba washing the feet of the poor, Wadia Park,
      Ahmednagar, India, September 12, 1954. Photographer:
      Panday. Courtesy of Meher Nazar Publications.

102   Meher Baba holding a goat in Alwar, India, February 1939.
      Photographer unknown. Courtesy of MSI Collection.

114   Meher Baba on a picnic, Trimbak, India, March 25, 1937.
      Rano and Freiny are holding Baba; Ruano is standing on
      the right. Photographer unknown. Courtesy of MSI
      Collection.

122   Meher Baba with Eruch at the Poona Center, Pune, India,
      May 1, 1965. Photographer: Meelan. Courtesy of Meher
      Nazar Publications.

128   Meher Baba, Bangalore, India, circa 1940. Photographer:
      Padri. Courtesy of Meher Nazar Publications.

140   Meher Baba feeding one of the *masts* at the Bangalore
      ashram, Bangalore, India, 1939. Photographer: Padri.
      Courtesy of Meher Nazar Publications.

152   Meher Baba feeding Lakhan Shah in the Rahuri Cabin,
      Lower Meherabad, India, early June 1939. Photographer:
      Padri. Courtesy of Meher Nazar Publications.

154   Meher Baba, Upper Meherabad, India, circa 1934-1935. Photographer: Mani. Courtesy of Meher Nazar Publications.

160   Mehera Irani, Upper Meherabad, India, circa 1938. Photographer unknown. Courtesy of Meher Nazar Publications.

178   Meher Baba with Gadge Maharaj and Pappa Jessawala, Wadia Park, Ahmednagar, India, September 12, 1954. Photographer: Nursoo or Panday. Courtesy of Meher Nazar Publications.

202   Meher Baba in Toka, India, 1928. Photographer unknown. Courtesy of Meher Nazar Publications.

220   Meher Baba with Naja, Mehera, and Khorshed, Upper Meherabad, India, July 8, 1936. Photographer: Mani. Courtesy of MSI Collection.

CPSIA information can be obtained
at www.ICGtesting.com
Printed in the USA
JSHW030315060222
22555JS00001B/1